CARTOONISTS
AT WAR

"RIGHT AGAINST WRONG."

CARTOONISTS AT WAR

Frank E. Huggett

WINDWARD

Windward

An imprint owned by

W. H. Smith & Son Ltd
Registered number: 237811 England

Trading as W H S Distributors,
St John's House,
East Street,
Leicester L E 1 6 N E

Produced by Guild Publishing
the Original Publications Division of
Book Club Associates

© Frank E. Huggett 1981

Designed by Tim Higgins

Set in Monophoto Plantin 110 and Grotesque 215
Printed and bound by Morrison & Gibb Ltd

Whilst every reasonable effort has been made to
find the copyright owners of the illustrations
in this book the publishers apologize to any
that they have been unable to trace and will
insert an acknowledgment in future editions
upon notification of the fact

ISBN 0 7112 0221 4

Frontispiece: A *Punch* cartoon published just
after the outbreak of the Crimean War

Endpapers:
Front: A contemporary cartoon of
the battle of Trafalgar
Back: A *Punch* cartoon from the First World War

CONTENTS

INTRODUCTION

The British sense of humour, which includes a healthy gift of laughing at oneself and a tendency to find foreigners hilariously funny, has always been one of the nation's greatest assets in time of war. For two centuries, caricaturists and cartoonists have helped the British to see the funny side of war by holding up their distorting mirror to misfortunes, both great and small, from the disastrous campaign of the Duke of York in Flanders and the invasion threats during the Napoleonic wars, through all the blunders of the old, incompetent generals in the Crimea, to the battered shins and bruises of the blackout in the Second World War. Cartoonists have created some of the most enduring fictional characters, who have come to symbolise whole eras of military history: the drawing room captain of early Victorian times; Lieutenant Plunger, of the cavalry, with his affected speech and anti-intellectual views; the testy, hookah-smoking colonel of the Indian army; Old Bill of the trenches; Colonel Blimp of the interwar years; Pilot Officer Prune, the Two Types, and Jane, who revealed her greatest potentialities during the Second World War to the delight of millions of servicemen. At the same time, cartoonists have always been the greatest champions of the nation's independence and freedom, mocking and reviling any foreign potentate, great or small, who posed a threat to British interests, from Napoleon to Hitler, and from King Kofi, the paramount chief of the Ashantis, to Cetewayo, the warrior-king of the Zulus.

But behind the laughter, there has usually been a far more serious purpose, too. Although Britain has been forced by necessity, honour, and pride into numerous wars in the last two hundred years, it has always had an ambiguous attitude towards its own defence. In times of war, there is scarcely any other nation which can be so patriotic, self-sacrificing, and proud of its armed forces; but, once peace has been declared, it quickly reverts to its traditional anti-militarist views again. Cartoonists have always reflected this love-hate relationship with the Services. Their work, which is concerned far more with feelings than with the underlying facts, presents a unique picture of the changing attitudes to the armed forces and of the British spirit in times of adversity.

The British spirit. A cavalry NCO and the regimental mascot pause between actions in the Middle East in the grim year of 1941

7

1

LITTLE BONEY

"My little friend Grildrig, you have made a most admirable "panegyric upon Yourself and Country, but from what I can "gather from your own relation & the answers I have with "much pains wringed & extorted from you, I cannot but con- "clude you to be, one of the most pernicious, little-odious- "reptiles, that nature ever sufferd to crawl upon the surface of the Earth."

The KING *of* BROBDINGNAG, *and* GULLIVER.

Vide *Swifts Gulliver* Voyage to Brobdingnag.

Previous page:
Gillray's derisive caricature
showing 'Little Boney' being
inspected by George III

Above: Napoleon gains
another of his great
victories at the battle of
Rivoli in 1797. A painting
by Philippoteaux

At the beginning of the war against revolutionary France in 1793, Britain was as usual ill-equipped and unprepared, trusting that a righteous God would somehow enable its army to muddle through in battles overseas and that its God-fearing navy would protect the island-home from invasion as it had done for so many centuries. With its long-lived aversion to a large standing army in peacetime and its traditional desire to get defence on the cheap, Britain had allowed its armed forces to wither away to an alarming extent in the ten years since the loss of the American colonies. No commander-in-chief had been appointed in the army, where corruption, nepotism, and officer-absenteeism were rife. Commissions and promotions up to the rank of lieutenant-colonel could all be purchased, except in the Royal Engineers and the Royal Artillery, so that some companies, and even some regiments, were commanded by children whose wealthy fathers had bought them real live soldiers as their playthings. Some captains were no more than twelve years of age; some lieutenant-colonels were still in their teens. In contrast, promotion in the navy was so slow that lieutenants often had to wait twenty years to get another ring, while promotion to flag rank took thirty or forty years.

Army officers had a general contempt for professionalism. In the more prestigious regiments, officers were far more concerned with cutting a dash in St James's than they were in dashing off to practise the arts of war, as we can still see in James Gillray's caricature, *Hero's Recruiting at Kelsey's,* a fashionable confectioner's in St James's Street, where four years after the outbreak of war, infant-officers were still stuffing themselves full of sugar plums. The dense stupidity of so many high-ranking army officers and their obvious liking for the good things of life, savagely etched out in *The Longitude and Latitude* of 1795, was one of the most common themes of caricaturists in the first few years of the war, when the general peacetime dislike of the army still prevailed.

With considerable justification, Georgian caricaturists and the general public had just as little respect for the common soldier. Many of them were in truth a sorry lot: penniless Irishmen, discharged prisoners, and half-witted drunkards, who had been plied with porter and promises of glory and adventure by some fast-talking recruiting sergeant in a beer house or a tavern. Privates received a miserable pittance of a shilling a day, out of which they had to buy all their own food, apart from bread, so that with enforced deductions from their pay, they were usually left with only a few pounds a year to spend on themselves. Undisciplined,

Caricaturists' views of the British army in the first years of the Napoleonic wars. Above: Typical, drunken army recruits as seen by the Suffolk caricaturist, Henry William Bunbury (1750–1811). Left: *The Longitude and Latitude* – the tall Marquis of Salisbury and the seventy-five-year-old Scottish General Grant, who was so keen on his food that he took his cook with him wherever he travelled. This caricature is probably the work of Isaac Cruikshank. Right: Gillray's savage attack on child captains and fashionable officers. 'Recruiting' is used here in the older sense of 'stuffing oneself with food'

J.G^s ad vivam fec^t. — Pub.^d June 9th 1797 by H. Humphrey, St James's Street

Hero's recruiting at Kelsey's; — or — Guard-Day at St James's.

and drunk whenever they could persuade some gullible civilian or relative to treat them, they were kept in line by the cat-o'-nine tails which was administered with great frequency in both peace and war. With so many incompetent and indifferent officers and such a rabble in the ranks, it was little wonder that morale in many regiments was very poor. Superior contempt was matched by an equally fierce resentment from below. A caricature called *A Military Extinguisher*, published just before the outbreak of the war, shows a tall soldier threatening to use his bearskin hat as a candle snuffer to extinguish his diminutive commanding officer. 'Be 'azy, child,' he growls, 'if you was not my commanding officer, I'd put you out.'

As in many subsequent wars, the first British campaign was almost a total disaster. An expeditionary force had been sent out to Flanders under the command of 'the grand old Duke of York', the second son of George III, whose incompetence as a field commander is still celebrated in the well-known nursery rhyme. After capturing the French stronghold of Valenciennes, he failed to press home his advantage by marching towards Paris, and wheeled instead to besiege Dunkirk; but within a few weeks the collapse of the Hanoverian army on his right and a lack of artillery forced him to abandon the siege. Although he was not entirely to blame, being handicapped by a lack of supplies and the disastrous strategy of the supreme allied commander, he did little to redeem his reputation in subsequent battles. Neither officers nor men covered themselves with glory in the campaign. The cavalry proved to be far more competent at slashing their own legs or their horse's ears than the enemy, and the infantry was often outmanoeuvred and outgunned by French skirmishers. The campaign continued for another nine months or so with increasing dissolution among the officers and increasing drunkenness, desertions, and deaths through disease and starvation among the men. The French captured Brussels on 10 July 1794, and Antwerp a few days later. The Duke of York first retreated with his forces into Germany and then in March 1795, he took them ignominiously back to England.

Shortly after the initial, and only, victory of the campaign at Valenciennes, Gillray had gone out to Flanders as the first officially-accredited war cartoonist. His main task, however, was to make some portrait sketches of the military commanders for the historical painter, Philippe-Jacques de Loutherbourg, who had been commissioned to paint a picture commemorating the victory. Gillray had already produced his own view of the expeditionary force and its

Gillray's caricature of 1793 shows the Duke of York supporting the weighty allurements of a Flemish courtesan on his knee, while emaciated guardsmen, on fatigues, bring in bowls of punch for the allied commanders

14

FATIGUES OF THE CAMPAIGN IN FLANDERS.

commander in *Fatigues of the Campaign in Flanders* and the sketches which he brought back from the front gave George III no greater pleasure.

Like gossip columnists of the present day, Georgian caricaturists were more often concerned with the private life of their victims than their public achievements and the Duke of York's love of women gave them many grounds for their truthfully based inventions. Later in the war the Duke's liaison with the notorious prostitute, Mary Anne Clarke, created an enormous scandal when it was revealed that she had been taking bribes on the pretext that she could secure army promotions through her influence on her lover. One of the first public hints of the affair had been given in Charles Williams's print, *The New Military Road to York by way of Frome,* of 1807. Frome was an agent for army commissions who was also implicated in the affair, and whose offices were shut shortly afterwards on the personal orders of the king.

Dozens of prints, many of them scatalogical, were issued by the printsellers. Although the Duke was exonerated by a parliamentary inquiry in 1809, the power of caricaturists to establish public images and to demolish private reputations was so great that we still see the unfortunate Duke through the eyes of Gillray, Cruikshank, and Thomas Rowlandson who produced a ribald print entitled *The Road to Preferment through Clarke's Passage.* Their attacks were based far more on imagination and innuendo than on detailed reason; their liberty to libel and distort was much greater than it has ever been since. Their exposure of the sins and failings of the wealthy and the powerful had a universal appeal, except for the victims and their friends, which has lasted to the present day. As a result, the Duke's great achievements as commander-in-chief in carrying out much-needed reforms in training, administration, organisation, and career structure, by setting a minimum age for promotion, have been almost as totally forgotten as de Loutherbourg's carefully-composed reconstruction of *The Grand Attack on Valenciennes.*

With the French invasions of Belgium, the Netherlands, the Rhineland, and northern Italy, Britain became increasingly vulnerable and isolated. Not for the last time in its history, Britain stood alone. The Prime Minister, Pitt, who believed, like many other politicians before and since, that he was a master of grand strategy, had already squandered the bulk of the small British army by sending it out to capture the French possessions in the West Indies, where about half of the eighty thousand troops died of disease. He now settled down to a long war of attrition with commando-style raids against French-held bases on the Continent and expeditions to other parts of the world where French interests could be threatened.

To pay for what was obviously going to be a much more lengthy conflict than had been anticipated, duties and taxes were increased; loyalty loans, the Georgian equivalent of post-war credits, were introduced; and fast days, which foreshadowed the purely secular rationing of the two world wars, were instituted, though, in Cruikshank's view, they made very little difference to the diet of Spitalfields weavers and other workers in declining industries who were already starving. Many of the taxes were designed to soak the rich, not through reforming zeal, but because they almost alone had any surplus money. A new tax on hair powder was introduced in 1795, which some employers evaded by forcing their powdered flunkeys to use ordinary flour instead, though the saving was soon eroded as the price of flour began to rise to previously unparalleled heights. In the following year the duty on wine went up by sixpence a bottle and a new dog tax was introduced. The next year, assessed taxes on such luxuries as carriages and male servants were trebled; a new tax was imposed on clocks and watches though it forced so many clockmakers out of business that it had to be repealed within twelve months; and a tax on men's hats was proposed which made some men start wearing caps instead. In 1799 there came the unkindest cut of all, from which the nation has never recovered, when an income tax was introduced at the savage rate of ten per cent which was not to be attained again until the middle of the First World War. Wartime austerity is by no means as new a problem as we may think.

The caricaturists, with their ribald wit, tried to make the victims of these crushing burdens smile at their misfortunes. George Murgatroyd Woodward showed one of the new breed of tax snoopers searching for unlicensed puppies in the voluminous skirts of a distressed lady, but bringing out a diminutive man instead. Later in the war, the financial burdens became even more oppressive when taxes were introduced or increased on many items including windows, malt, soap, candles, salt, tobacco, and home-brewed beer. Gillray shows Charles James Fox, the former 'Friend of the People' knocking demandingly at the front door of a poor, harassed John Bull who has been forced to shut up his shop and to move upstairs where he lives on the menial tasks of cleaning other people's shoes and carrying parcels. With all the self-righteous unction which has long been the hallmark of the successful politician, Fox is saying persuasively: 'Taxes must be had Johnny. Come down with your cash. It's all for the good of your dear country', an appeal to which citizens have been increasingly subject ever since. This ability of the Georgian cartoonists to identify the course of future trends has given their best work an enduring strength.

As in many later conflicts, the first response of the patriotic 'benevolent ladies of Great Britain' to the war had been to clothe their 'modern heroes' in flannel pants and waistcoats. Many mocking prints were produced about these often ill-fitting complements, with such titles as *Flannel Coats of Mail against the Cold*. At the same time as society ladies started to

MATERNAL LOVE.

The Fashionable Mamma, — or — The Convenience of Modern Dress. Vide The Pocket Hole, &c.

wrap up their men's vital parts as warmly as a baby's, they started to reveal their own to public view. Not for another hundred and fifty years were women's clothes to be again so revealing or so convenient for *The Fashionable Mamma* who could use the vestigial traces of pockets which appeared as slits in her flimsy dress to give her baby instant nourishment. As the necklines dropped lower and lower, the plumes of ostrich feathers in the coiled and braided hair rose ever higher. The low necklines and the see-through dresses attracted many appraising glances and ribald remarks from servicemen. As John Cawse makes a sailor say in his *Nautical Observations on Female Dress:* 'Women are like crazy hulks in a rough sea; the portholes are hardly secure.' To which his friend replies: 'Or like great guns. Long and lank.'

For almost a whole decade, from 1795 to 1805, Britain had to live with dark fears of invasion. The main home defence force in times of emergency was the militia, which since the middle of the eighteenth century had been raised by compulsory ballot, though richer men who were unlucky enough to be selected were allowed to pay a substitute to serve in their place. To augment these forces, Pitt appealed for 60,000 volunteers – a supplementary militia – to undertake twenty days' training. In all parts of the country, men rushed to join the Georgian equivalent of 'Dad's Army'. At first, the caricaturists did not take these new forces very seriously. Gillray showed these ill-assorted bands of 'St George's volunteers' charging determinedly with fixed bayonets, not at the French, but down Bond Street after 'storming the dunghill at Marybone'. Outside the cities, farmers polished up their spurs and stripped their walls of muskets and blunderbusses and their sheds of flails and pitchforks, but this bucolic cavalry fared no better at the caricaturists' hands. As they practise their charges on carthorses, a blast of slugs sends some pigeons to a premature death, a frightened farm labourer takes refuge in a well, and old ladies are thrown violently to the ground. Decrepit squires, attracted by the bait of military rank, formed their own independent companies of fencibles, paid soldiers on home service for the duration, who were dismissed disparagingly by Isaac Cruikshank as 'Suffolk rats protecting their cheese'.

Their contemptuous attitude to volunteer auxiliary forces in the first stages of the conflict, when all its potential dangers had not been fully realised, was to be repeated by other cartoonists in later wars, reflecting the basic national concern to remain isolated from land wars as long as possible.

Women's revealing styles and extravagant head-dresses were satirised by Gillray in this caricature of 1796

There were many other light-hearted caricatures during the first invasion scare. Isaac Cruikshank makes an attractive young girl say to a repressed old harridan:

> – I do assure you I did not close a leg (an Eye, I mean) all last night.
> – Why really, Miss you surprise me . . . Do you think they will *ravish us all*!!!

But there were other would-be fraternisers who posed a far more serious threat to the safety of the nation – a small group of influential MPs led by Charles James Fox who were initially sympathetic to the revolutionary ideals of the French people. The caricaturists had no time for this 'fifth column' which was attacked by Gillray in several prints, including the *French-Telegraph making Signals in the Dark*. Gillray's devastating attack had a considerable effect in turning public opinion against Fox, who saw events in terms of narrow intellectual idealism. Gillray's views, on the other hand, were based on more emotionally appealing, patriotic, and humanitarian feelings which in the end, through his political prescience, proved to be far more valid.

Naval skills and audacity – and the weather – combined to

FRENCH-TELEGRAPH making SIGNALS in the Dark.

James Gillray (1757–1815) was the most intense and powerful of all British caricaturists. He was born in Chelsea, the son of a Scottish soldier, and after being apprenticed to a letter-head engraver, he studied at the Royal Academy schools. His first major success came in 1786 with *A New Way to Pay the National Debt* – a satire on the Royal Family who remained one of his favourite targets for caricature. He continued with his attacks on royalty, dishonest politicians, and the establishment in general after the outbreak of war with revolutionary France; but, as a great lover of liberty, he was even more scathing and scurrilous in his attacks on Napoleon.

Gillray produced about 1,500 caricatures, most of which were published by Hannah Humphrey of St James's Street, an elderly, bespectacled spinster who had assumed the courtesy title of 'Mrs'. He lodged – or lived – with her from 1797. His powers of draughtsmanship, his grotesque imagination, and the strength of his convictions made him one of the great masters of caricature of all times. He was fearless in his attacks on incompetence, pretension, and hypocrisy wherever they were to be found; but he remained a true patriot and a great supporter of the common man. Gillray's career was abruptly terminated by insanity four years before his death in 1815.

Left: Charles James Fox, who sympathised initially with the French revolution, is seen by Gillray as the recently-invented French telegraph, guiding the invasion fleet to St Paul's Cathedral

defeat the first French attempts at invasion. The French struck at the weakest flank, Ireland, which was then seething with rebellion. The United Irishmen under Wolfe Tone had appealed for French assistance in their short-lived struggle for independence. In December 1796, a French invasion fleet carrying 15,000 troops, put out from Brest, but it was scattered by fierce gales in Bantry Bay, off County Cork, before it could land. It was not only Ireland which was simmering with revolt. Many sailors, the first line of defence against invasion, were up in arms about the poor quality of their food, their lack of shore leave and medical care, and particularly their wages which had not been increased for nearly 150 years! In 1797, their discontent flared into open mutiny at Spithead and the Nore. The Admiralty quelled these mutinies by a combination of concessions and firmness, but only just in time as within a few months a Dutch fleet, who were by then allies of the French, set sail to bring help to the Irish. It was defeated by the former mutineers commanded by Lord Duncan at Camperdown off the Dutch coast. By the time the French eventually put a small force of 1,000 men ashore at Killala Bay in August 1798, the Irish rebellion had been crushed and the French invaders were soon rounded up by the British army.

In the same month there was renewed proof of the

enduring supremacy of the Royal Navy when Nelson gained one of his most brilliant and audacious victories in the battle of the Nile, which restored British control of the Mediterranean again for the duration of the war. When he found the French fleet anchored in Aboukir Bay off the Egyptian coast, he ordered some of his ships to sail into the shoal water, even though it was already getting dark, so that he could attack from both the land and the seaward sides. After an engagement which went on all night, only two French ships of the line escaped unscathed. When the news of this momentous victory reached England, there was immense jubilation: the Royal Navy had proved its worth and its valour yet again. Gillray pictured Nelson up to his knees in water extirpating 'the revolutionary crocodiles' or 'the plague of Egypt' with a stout cudgel of British oak. Another print shows a tousled John Bull of enormous girth – 'old grumble gizzard' eating a French 'frigasee', while a group of victorious British admirals including Nelson, Howe, Bridport, and Duncan offer him further frigates and warships for his feast. 'Why, you sons of bitches, you,' he grumbles jocularly, 'where do ye think I shall find room to stow all you bring in.'

By this time, Napoleon, who had already established his reputation as the most brilliant French general, had already started to appear in English caricatures; but it was only after he had overthrown the Directory in 1799 and had been appointed First Consul, or virtual dictator, that the caricaturists started to treat him as the main enemy. In the following fifteen years at least 2,000 caricatures of him were published. He was depicted in as many disparaging and contemptuous guises as the involved imaginations of the British caricaturists could devise: a caged animal; the devil incarnate with horns protruding through the famous cocked hat; a Corsican bloodhound being savaged by a sturdy British bulldog; a voyeur peering at his future first wife, Josephine, dancing in the nude behind a filmy net of gauze. But it was Gillray's conception of 'Little Boney' which captured the public imagination most strongly by helping to cut down his significance and his achievements to a defeatable size. In *The King of Brobdingnag and Gulliver,* Gillray shows a full-size George III peering through a monocular at the Lilliputian figure of Napoleon on his hand and pronouncing him to be 'one of the most pernicious, little odious reptiles, that nature ever suffer'd to crawl upon the surface of the Earth'. Contempt and vituperation did not come in small sizes in those more robust times.

The propaganda value of these pictorial attacks was

immense. Just as the caricaturists relied for their basic outlines on the orthodox, engraved portraits of Napoleon which had first reached England from Italy in 1797, so did the general public, in those days of non-pictorial newspapers, depend to a considerable extent on the caricaturists' exaggerations for their vision of distant personalities and events. The windows of the London printsellers attracted great crowds of inquisitive spectators of all classes to view Gillray's or Rowlandson's latest work. There was always such a great crush around Mrs Humphrey's in St James's Street, Rudolph Ackermann's in the Strand, Thomas Tegg's in Cheapside, and John Hatchard's and Samuel William Fores's in Piccadilly that the latter had to have an iron railing put up before his window to hold back the crowds. Portfolios of coloured caricatures were let out by the evening for the diversion of fashionable society, while the plain versions were cheap enough to be bought and exhibited in shops and taverns or even for display on the walls of relatively humble homes. The influence of caricatures on public attitudes was greater during the Napoleonic wars than it has ever been since, partly because the supreme masters of the art – Gillray, Rowlandson, the Cruikshanks, and many others – were then at the height of their powers.

There was a temporary lull in the conflict with France and much unthinking and premature jubilation when the Peace of Amiens was signed on 27 March 1802; but the caricaturists, more practised in the realistic, or cynical, assessment of political and diplomatic motive, were less deceived than many members of the public. Although a few flattering caricatures of Napoleon were produced, suspicions of the French dictator remained as indelibly etched in their minds as on the majority of prints. This brief, uneasy reconciliation, symbolised in Gillray's *The First Kiss this Ten Years*, made hostility and hatred even more intense when the war flared up again in May 1803. Napoleon was almost immediately depicted in his more usual role again, as a madman whose 'ravings' had upset the globe which lies broken near his feet, while he stamps and rages 'in a strong Fit'. Caricaturists raked up grossly exaggerated stories of Napoleon's past atrocities. It was alleged that during his Middle Eastern campaign of 1798–9, he had ordered Turkish prisoners to be slaughtered, even though they had surrendered on the understanding that they would be spared, and that he had ordered French soldiers, stricken with the plague, to be drugged to death with opium by the doctors who were treating them.

With Napoleon firmly in command and determined to

invade England, British fears increased. People remembered Gillray's grim prediction made five years before of what the *Consequences of a Successful French Invasion* might be: the House of Commons stripped of its mace and with pairs of fettered MPs awaiting transportation to Botany Bay; the thrones of the House of Lords replaced by the guillotine; and ragged English men and women toiling as labourers in the fields beneath the long French whip and the needle-pointed goad. The increased fears produced a radical change in the caricaturists' attitude to volunteers. No longer were they depicted as bucolic buffoons, but as stout-hearted citizens, the new heroes of the day, making their *Resolutions in case of an Invasion,* with the barber threatening to 'lather the whiskers' of Napoleon and the publican to 'cool his courage in a pot of Brown Stout'. Isaac Cruikshank tried to increase the morale of his compatriots, whose traditional diet consisted of roast beef and suet puddings, by assuring them that Napoleon had never come up against anything more substantial than 'macaroni and sour crout' before, using the emotional appeal of national foods to arouse pride and xenophobic feelings. Other caricaturists showed country wives plundering the bodies of defeated French invaders and complaining that all they could find was garlic, onions, and 'a parcel of pill boxes', while their volunteer husbands triumphantly exhibited the decapitated heads of French soldiers on their pikes. There was a large measure of wish fulfilment in these caricatures, as it is extremely doubtful if the 400,000 volunteers in Great Britain and Ireland would have been much of a match for seasoned French troops. The spirit may have been there, but not the weapons. It was revealed in a debate in the House in 1803 that some 120,000 volunteers were still waiting to be issued with muskets and were forced to make do with pikes and pitchforks, as was to happen again in the early years of the Home Guard during the Second World War.

By the summer of 1805 Napoleon, who was by then the Emperor of France, had assembled a vast invasion force of 90,000 men and 2,000 transports near Boulogne and at other Channel ports. At one time, he had hoped to send the whole of his invasion force across the Channel on one calm night; but this scheme, like many others was abandoned, mainly through fears of British naval might. Impatient for action of some sort, Napoleon had given up his plans for invasion and set off on a long forced march to deal with the resurgent Austrians seven weeks before Nelson's victory at Trafalgar on 21 October 1805, finally laid to rest Napoleon's threats, and established British command of the seas for a century.

Gillray's satire of the Peace of Amiens, 1802, which brought a brief respite in the war between England and France

The first Kiſs this Ten Years! __ or __ the meeting of Britannia & Citizen François

Nelson's decisive defeat of the combined French and Spanish fleets off the southern coasts of Spain confirmed all Napoleon's suspicions and fears that the French were no match for the British at sea.

When the first reports of the great victory at Trafalgar reached Britain sixteen days later, the nation's joy was overshadowed by the news that Nelson had been killed as he stood on deck in his full-dress uniform with his many decorations glittering on his chest, an obvious, if not easy, target for any sniper. Nelson's body was brought back to England in January 1806, to lie in state for three days in the Painted Chamber at Greenwich Hospital, before it was taken up river in a barge procession for burial in St Paul's Cathedral. He had been loved not only by the civilian

A contemporary cartoon showing a British warship being boarded by the French and Spanish during the battle of Trafalgar. In fact, this incident never occurred, but was invented by the caricaturist

population and the officers who served under him but also, more unusually in those days, by all the men who sailed with him. Although the Admiralty had the good sense to include some of the *Victory's* complement of 628 men in the waterborne procession, the ecclesiastical authorities of St Paul's, with an un-Christian meanness of spirit, decided to charge all visitors, including sailors, twopence to see Nelson's tomb. Their meanness was satirised by Woodward, who shows a sailor standing beside his own monument to 'his Noble companion' which he had constructed in his own back garden out of his old sea chest, two kegs of grog, and an Englishman's heart draped with crepe.

While Britain remained victorious at sea, the French still triumphed on the land, smashing the Austrians and the Russians at Austerlitz on 2 December 1805, and the Prussians at Jena and Auerstadt less than a year later. Napoleon then turned his restless attention to the other side of Europe, putting his elder brother on the Spanish throne and invading Portugal. It was there, in the Iberian peninsula, that the British, after some initial waverings, decided to launch their main land attack against the French. The Peninsular War was long and arduous, lasting from 1808 to 1814, with numerous setbacks and reverses and enforced withdrawals into the safer base of Portugal to regroup and to amass fresh supplies. The British army was outnumbered by at least five to one by the huge French army of conscripts which totalled 250,000 men for most of the time. Britain, with its long-standing, traditional opposition to conscription, found it difficult to obtain sufficient recruits, particularly as they were then forced to enlist for life, as a twenty-one years' engagement was not introduced until 1847. Some of the gaps in the ranks were filled by volunteers from the home militia who had responded to government appeals for them to serve overseas; but service as an army private still had very little appeal.

In a different way, the army was not much more attractive as a career to keen young subalterns, who were often overburdened by debt through the purchase of their commission and the obligatory social expenses of regimental life and who normally found it difficult to get promotion unless they had the right name or connections or sufficient fortune to buy advancement. The trials, tribulations, and eventual triumph, by other means, of a young 'sub' in the Peninsular War were depicted in a series of coloured aquatints by Rowlandson, which provides an illuminating picture of the wartime experiences of a typical young officer at the time. They were used to illustrate 'The Military

Adventures of Johnny Newcome', a long, cautionary tale in verse written under the pseudonym of 'Officer' by Lieutenant-Colonel David Roberts, which might equally well have been entitled 'How to succeed in the army without really trying'.

We first encounter Johnny Newcome, the common name for a newly-joined officer, riding towards his new life in Portugal with high hopes and an eager, steadfast look, and followed on foot by his red-nosed, pipe-smoking Irish batman, a typical army scrounger if there ever was one. On arrival in Lisbon, Johnny first pays a visit to 'Senior' Cavigoli, a profiteering dealer in Army stores, to lay in a stock of provisions from his wide range of food and drink which includes 'Hollands, Genebra and pickled tripes'. When Johnny reaches the billet which has been allotted to him by a Portuguese magistrate, he is greeted with such ferocity by the snarling peasants who are gathered round the open fire in their dismal, barely-furnished room, that he decides to lodge at a wineshop at his own expense instead.

When he reaches his regiment after another long ride, he is welcomed by his long-nosed colonel in an off-hand, rather disparaging way. It is not long before Johnny 'smells powder for the first time'. When his captain is killed, he is ordered to lead the men into battle, without, of course, being given any promotion. Their victory over the French is celebrated not

Below: Johnny Newcome, on the right of the advancing line, leads his men into action

Smells Powder for the first time.

with a banquet, but with half-rations which consist mainly of 'flinty biscuit' and 'tough and stinking beef', though his batman somehow manages to scrounge half a loaf of bread from somewhere. Exhausted by the meagre diet and the hot pursuit of the French, Johnny succumbs to a fever and is taken back to Lisbon in an ox-cart for repatriation so that he can recuperate.

He arrives home to find his father, a former grocer grown so rich on profiteering that he has become a banker, a City alderman, and an MP. Johnny decides that hard cash is a quicker road to success than hard campaigning and allows his father to buy him a captaincy in one of the Guards regiments, which brings about a wondrous improvement in his career and life. On his return to Lisbon he is entertained by the British envoy and is given a sealed letter to present to Wellington, who appoints him an extra ADC. Our last glimpse of Johnny comes in London, where he has returned to present the Prince Regent with Joseph Bonaparte's crown and Marshal Jourdan's baton on behalf of Wellington. As a reward for those arduous services, he is knighted and promoted lieutenant-colonel, and his proud father makes him an MP by buying him a seat in parliament. Of such stern stuff were many Army 'heroes' made, while, in contrast, as the officer-author of Johnny Newcome points out, there were many 'gallant fellows' like Lieutenant Dyar, of the 51st

Thomas Rowlandson (1756–1827) was a far more distinguished draughtsman than most British caricaturists and cartoonists, but his work sometimes lacks the 'bite' of other less able artists. Born in London, he went to Paris at the age of sixteen to study at the Académie Royale school. On his return he studied at the Royal Academy schools in London. He started out as a painter of portraits and serious subjects and exhibited at the Royal Academy from 1775. Rowlandson had been left £7,000 by an aunt, a considerable sum of money in those days; but he was an inveterate gambler and he soon squandered his legacy. To pay his debts, and to make a living, he turned to social caricature in about 1780. His reputation as a witty commentator on the social scene was firmly established by *Vauxhall Gardens* in 1784.

He travelled all over England, and also in France, Germany, and the Low Countries, making sketches of country life and of fashionable society. Much of his work was published by Ackermann, including the famous series entitled *The Miseries of Life,* 1808, and *The Tours of Dr Syntax,* 1812–20. His best work is distinguished by its flowing draughtsmanship and his rollicking sense of humour.

Light Regiment, who had twice led successful storming parties as a volunteer, but still remained a 'sub'.

Out of this diverse material, Wellington, who was in command for most of the time, forged a victorious army, indeed Britain's only real army of the war. Unlike Marlborough or Nelson, he inspired more fear than affection in his junior officers and men. He achieved his results by iron discipline, aloof command, and punctilious attention to detail.

Wellington eventually provided some victories on land for both soldiers and civilians to cheer. French losses at the battle of Salamanca on 22 July 1812, were almost three times as high as the British. This victory opened the way to Madrid which was taken by Wellington on 12 August. Back home, Charles Williams depicted Napoleon's brother, 'King Joey' dressed in his royal robes, and carrying a bag of plunder over his shoulder, fleeing from the avenging Wellington. There was even greater jubilation in the following year when the French lost all their transport and artillery at Vitoria, the last major battle on Spanish soil. London was illuminated for three nights. A print by the twenty-one-year-old George Cruikshank shows Wellington on his white horse gazing down in triumph at a pile of trophies and exclaiming, 'Why, here's enough for three nights' illuminations,' to which one of his aides replies, 'Three times three, my Lord!'

It was not only in the Iberian peninsula that Napoleon's star was waning. His disastrous decision to invade Russia was one of the main reasons for his eventual downfall. With truly remarkable speed, Napoleon had advanced across Russia, taking Vilna, defeating the Russians at Smolensk, and fighting a savage battle at Borodino, 110 kilometres west of Moscow, with heavy casualties on both sides. The Russians retreated in defeat, but not in total disarray. After thirteen weeks, Napoleon entered Moscow only to discover an inferno as the Russians has set fire to three-quarters of the city. For over a month, Napoleon waited there impatiently, hoping that the Russians would sue for peace, before he decided too late to retire to winter quarters. As in later wars, Russia's greatest ally, 'General Winter' came to its aid. The frost came hard and early that year, and the French suffered terribly on their retreat. Poorly-clothed, frost-bitten, and starving, they disembowelled horses which had died from the cold and crept into them at night to seek refuge from the icy, snow-laden wind and the twenty degrees of frost. Of the 500,000 men who had marched on Moscow, only 20,000 returned.

During the retreat, Napoleon might have been captured by a band of Cossacks had they not been turned away to loot some undefended French waggons. The Cossacks became the new heroes of the day in England. William Elmes captured the general feeling of delight at their success in his *Cossack Sports* which shows them in hot pursuit of a Corsican fox with the face and the huge cocked hat of Napoleon, and in the *Cossack Extinguisher* in which a fearsome-looking, bearded Cossack, armed with a pair of pistols, a sword, and a long lance, is about to extinguish the diminutive figure of Napoleon with his fur cap. There was immense excitement when two representative Cossacks in their dark blue jackets, baggy trousers, and tall fur caps visited London in April 1813, in a gesture of wartime goodwill and solidarity. One of the Cossacks gave a demonstration of his skills on horseback in Hyde Park which delighted the great crowds of spectators.

On his return to France, Napoleon demanded 350,000 conscripts to replace his shattered *Grande Armée*. When it became known that these included children the indignation at this extension of warfare to the schoolroom knew no bounds. George Cruikshank sarcastically depicted Napoleon trying to induce his 'pretty little Heroes' to return with him to the Russian front: 'There you shall see the dancing bears and play at snowballs, and you shall get all the nice sugar-plums, and if you behave yourselves like good children you may perhaps get a pair of pretty wooden legs.'

Napoleon was now faced by a far more resolute fourth coalition supported, or bribed, as he would have claimed, by English gold, consisting of Sweden, Russia, Prussia, Austria, Bavaria and, at the eleventh hour, Wurtemburg and Saxony. The ensuing battle of Leipzig lasted for three days from 16 October to 19 October 1813. The French fought bravely, but they were outnumbered, their lines of supply were long, and the terrain gave Napoleon few opportunities to display his tactical skills. It was the first battle he had personally commanded and lost. When he retreated, he left behind half of his army, many of them captured or drowned when a bridge across the Elster, the only escape route, was blown up prematurely by mistake.

With the remorseless advance of the allied armies towards the French frontier, and the uprisings of the formerly subject peoples from Bavaria in the south to the Netherlands in the north, Napoleon became increasingly isolated, an emperor in search of a lost empire and military might. On 1 January 1814, the Prussian army under Marshal Blücher crossed the Rhine and before the end of the month, battles were raging on French soil. Within four months Napoleon had abdicated. His second wife, Marie Louise, the daughter

THE DEVILS DARLING.

Anti-Napoleon caricatures. Left: Rowlandson's version of 1814 which was copied from a German original, and (right) George Cruikshank's celebration of Napoleon's departure for Elba

of the Austrian Emperor, and their young son, were captured by allied soldiers. In despair Napoleon tried to commit suicide by taking a dose of opium and belladonna which his doctor had prepared for him during the Russian campaign; but because Napoleon, with his boastful pride, had insisted that it should be strong enough to kill two men, his body rejected the poison which he vomited out.

With his immense vitality and his powerful constitution, Napoleon had recovered, physically and psychologically, by the following day. After attending a farewell parade of his Old Guard at Fontainebleau, he was conducted to the small island of Elba which the Allies had given him to rule as emperor. He was taken into captivity in an English frigate and not in the iron cage as his depressed forebodings had prompted him to imagine during the retreat from Moscow; but that was how George Cruikshank, who must have probed down to the same level of atavistic imagination, pictured his departure to Elba.

The Cruikshanks – Isaac (*c.* 1756–1811), and his sons, **Robert** (1789–1856) and **George** (1792–1878) – were Britain's most talented family of caricaturists. The most famous was **George,** (above), who had no formal training as an artist, but who picked up all he needed to know in his artistic home. While he was still in his teens, he started to publish brilliant political caricatures, and his attacks on Napoleon, and on the private life of the Prince Regent, brought him early fame. He contributed to many of the satirical magazines which proliferated in the early decades of the nineteenth century, the *Scourge* from 1811–6, the *Meteor,* 1813–4, and *The Humorist,* 1819–21. In the 1820s he turned to book illustration, on which his reputation now mainly rests. His best illustrations include those for Grimm's *German Popular Stories,* 1823–6, and *Fairy Tales,* 1827; Dickens's *Sketches by Boz* and *Oliver Twist;* and Ainsworth's *The Tower of London.* In latter life he published many pictorial attacks on spiritualism and drunkenness.

Robert Cruikshank started work as a midshipman with the East India Company, but soon gave up the sea for an artist's life. He produced many social and political caricatures, and also illustrated books dealing with the social foibles of London life. Isaac, the father, was a prolific caricaturist and water-colourist, who exhibited at the Royal Academy and designed the frontispiece for the *Witticisms and Jests of Dr Samuel Johnson.*

The HEbbEL BARONIAN Emperor going to take possession of his new Territory.

Within a year, Napoleon had escaped from his island prison, and was installed in Paris again, the French king, Louis XVIII having fled ignominiously to Belgium. Caricaturists blamed the interminable wrangling among the allied representatives at the Congress of Vienna, or the Congress of Blockheads as George Cruikshank unkindly called it, with its frivolous emphasis on protracted banquets and balls, for Napoleon's resurgence. But his second coming was short-lived. In celebration of Waterloo, William Heath published a valedictory caricature, *A Lecture on Heads*, showing Wellington killing a French soldier with his sword while Blücher exhibits a decapitated head on the point of his sabre. This time, the Allies made sure that Napoleon should never repeat his escapade, by banishing him to the remote island of St Helena in the South Atlantic, where, guarded by over 2,000 soldiers at great expense to his enemies, he died in 1821 at the age of fifty-one.

The general jubilation and sense of relief at the final defeat of the Corsican 'usurper' were overshadowed by feelings of pity and sorrow at the human costs of the long conflict which had been necessary to bring about his downfall. Throughout the war, caricaturists had always been conscious of the waste and folly of war. Death lurks in the corner of many of their most striking and famous productions, and its skeletal figure was their shorthand symbol for the waste of war, a pictorial tradition stretching back to the middle ages. During the 'Hundred Days' Rowlandson had depicted Napoleon on the balcony of the Tuileries with the skeletal finger of death pointing towards the exultant crowds below while earlier, after the battle of Leipzig, he had used the same symbolism in his famous caricature, *The Two Kings of Terror*, in which a defeated Napoleon tries to read the riddle of triumphant death. At a more individual level, many other caricaturists had protested against the waste of war. In the first few months of the war, Gillray, whose father had lost an arm while serving in Flanders as a private during the War of the Austrian Succession, published an anti-war caricature, *John Bull's Progess*, showing a prosperous countryman setting out for war and returning as a ragged cripple to his starving family. A similar story in seven scenes, instead of four, was told by Cruikshank in *He Would be a Soldier*, which was published shortly afterwards. It was a theme to which caricaturists were to return time and time again during subsequent years; but their appeals to finer feelings have usually had much less impact than their witty comments on the depravities and deficiencies of their own age. By its nature, the caricature is essentially an ephemeral art. The

Napoleon, with the imperial standard lying broken at his feet, confronts the skeletal figure of death after his defeat at Leipzig

T. Rowlandson del.

COPY

OF THE

Transparency

EXHIBITED AT

ACKERMANN'S REPOSITORY OF ARTS,

During the Illuminations of the 5th and 6th of November, 1813,

IN HONOUR OF THE SPLENDID VICTORIES OBTAINED BY

The ALLIES over the ARMIES of FRANCE,

AT LEIPSIC AND ITS ENVIRONS.

THE TWO KINGS OF TERROR.

THIS Subject, representing the two Tyrants, viz. the Tyrant BONAPARTE and the Tyrant DEATH, sitting together on the Field of Battle, in a manner which promises a more perfect intimacy immediately to ensue, is very entertaining. It is also very instructing to observe, that the former is now placed in a situation in which all Europe *may see through him.* The emblem, too, of the Circle of dazzling light from mere *vapour*, which is so *soon extinguished*, has a good moral effect; and as the Gas represents the dying flame, so does the Drum, on which he is seated, typify the *hollow* and *noisy* nature of the falling Usurper.

The above description of the subject appeared in the *Sun* of Saturday, the 6th of November. These pointed comments arose from the picture being *transparent*, and from a Circle, indicative of the strength and brotherly union of the Allies, which surmounted the same, composed of *gas* of brilliant brightness.

Georgian caricaturists remained creatures of their own times and had their greatest impact on their contemporaries through their exposure of the corruption of court life, the scandals of high society, and the hypocritical attitudes of politicians. Through great draughtsmanship and the universal appeal of their passion and humour, their work was occasionally transformed into something of enduring worth, but much of it was as transient as a light perfume, recalling the atmosphere and feelings of lost days, but lacking any great substance.

2

BRITANNIA RULES THE WAVES

SHARP'S THE WORD.

ADMIRAL PUNCH'S SIGNAL TO THE FLEET.

Britain emerged triumphant from the Napoleonic wars as the most powerful nation on earth, with its empire expanded by many strategically important acquisitions, including the Cape of Good Hope, Malta, and Ceylon; its army victorious, even though the last battle had in Wellington's words been 'the nearest-run thing'; and its navy the strongest the world had ever seen. But people were far less concerned with pride in these achievements than in the price they had paid, and continued to pay, to make them possible. As the new generals of Cruikshank's 'peace establishment' – General Complaint, General Bankruptcy, and General Starvation – took command, there was general agitation for cuts in government spending. One of the prime targets, as it had been after almost every major war, was defence. In *The British Atlas*, Charles Williams shows a Churchillian-looking John Bull, with patched trousers and pockets empty of everything but unpaid bills, supporting a standing army of 150,000 men, while in the background the Royal Navy maintains its guard on Napoleon who is kept prisoner on St Helena at a cost to the taxpayer of £300,000 a year. The demands of retrenchment soon resulted in British troops being brought back from France and in the Navy being slashed to the smallest size for almost a century. In 1813, the navy had had over 1,000 ships and 130,000 men; but four years later there were less than 200 ships and 23,000 sailors. The Admiralty, hardpressed for money and with its continuing reverence for the old 'wooden walls' which had kept England safe from invasion for so many years, was reluctant to modernise the fleet, so that it was left to France, seeking to redeem the honour it had lost in the Napoleonic wars, to pioneer steam propulsion instead of sail, and to develop iron warships and armoured plate.

Nevertheless, the prestige of the Royal Navy was still so high that its supremacy remained unchallenged for many years. The navy lived on its reputation, its skills in seamanship, its iron discipline, and its individual acts of bravery and initiative, often in defiance of orders, which have always made the reputations of so many of its great commanders. The Nelson touch was not a myth but a living reality. In 1816, for example, when Captain Murray Maxwell sailed the *Alceste* up the River Canton without Chinese permission and a line of war junks opened fire, he impudently took it as a welcoming salute, which he promptly returned, sailing on unabashed and unchecked, through a hail of fire from Chinese forts on both banks of the river, until he reached the largest battery which he silenced with a

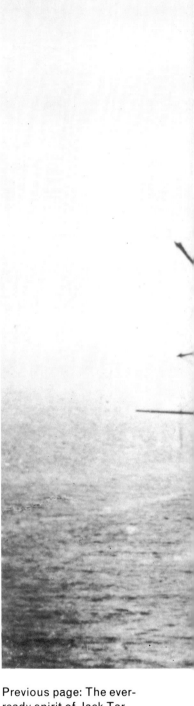

Previous page: The ever-ready spirit of Jack Tar as pictured by *Punch*

Above: Warships of
the Channel Squadron in
the late 1840s

single broadside. It was undaunted, reckless courage of this kind which made the navy what it was and enabled it to act as the world's policeman for much of the nineteenth century. Its ships sailed into all the oceans of the world carrying its message of freedom – of the seas, of trade, and of subject nations, unless they happened to be British colonies or enemies.

The navy carried on a ceaseless crusade against the slave trade and piracy, which were sometimes intermingled. Britain had abolished the slave trade in 1807 and in the next few years many other maritime powers, including the United States, did the same; but the profits were so great that it continued to flourish illegally. By treaty arrangements with other nations, and occasionally without, the Royal Navy stopped and boarded any vessels suspected of carrying slaves. It was so successful in this task, freeing nearly 150,000 slaves in just over fifty years, that the Admiralty was forced to reduce the bounty for each freed male slave from £60 to £5.

It was just as active in the worldwide fight against pirates. Algiers, one of the main bases for the Barbary pirates, who

Right: After the Napoleonic wars, there were immediate civilian howls for cuts in defence spending, epitomised in Charles Williams's cartoon of 1816

Below: British sailors teaching pirates a lesson in international law

BRITISH SAILOR'S. BOARDING AN ALGERINE PIRATE.

THE BRITISH ATLAS, or John Bull supporting the Peace Establishment.

had harassed merchant ships in the Mediterranean since the sixteenth century, was bombarded by a squadron under Admiral Lord Exmouth on 27 August 1816, with such devastating effect that the following morning the Bey of Algiers promptly agreed to release all Christian slaves and to free the British consul who had been imprisoned. The navy continued to take punitive action against the Algerian pirates until the French occupation of the city in 1830 started to curtail their activities. It was not only in the Mediterranean that the Royal Navy carried out its self-appointed task as the guardian of international law. No pirates were safe from its challenge from the Persian Gulf to Malaya, from the West Indies to China, and from West Africa to Borneo, where on 1 July 1849, a large force of pirates in 120 canoe-shaped proas were exterminated in a particularly nasty way – some of them being churned to death in the water by the paddle wheels of one of the attacking naval vessels.

The navy's reputation enabled it to act as the arbiter in the fate of many smaller nations so that it played a major part in helping the Greeks to achieve independence from Turkish rule. The Greek cause had attracted great support in Britain from philhellenic liberals such as Lord Byron and from mercenaries such as Lord Cochrane, a naval captain, dismissed from the service for alleged fraud, who had earlier helped the infant republics of Latin America in their struggle for freedom. But the Royal Navy did more to help the Greeks gain their independence when a combined fleet of British, French, and Russian warships under Vice-Admiral Sir Edward Codrington decisively defeated the Turkish fleet at the battle of Navarino Bay on 20 October 1827. Not everyone in Britain welcomed the victory. Some people feared that the further weakening of Turkey might encourage the Russians to seize Constantinople; but the liberal rejoicing at the creation of another free state was expressed by William Heath in a cartoon published shortly after the news of the victory had reached London. He shows a grateful Greek asking a jovial British sailor if they can count upon further aid to which the sailor happily replies: 'To be sure you can – and here's my Messmates who will stick to you as long as we have a Timber afloat.' His high-minded confidence epitomised the general attitudes of the British public towards the nineteenth-century navy as the prime defender of worldwide freedom, a view which was to be reflected in many subsequent cartoons.

Naval power was used in a far more arbitrary way by Lord Palmerston, the hero of so many Victorian cartoons, who dominated foreign policy from 1830 to his death in 1865. He

EXTRAORDINARY GAZETTE. Saturday November 10 1827.

ADMIRAL CODRINGTON & his ALLIES *lending the* BRAVE GREEKS *a hand & teaching the* OTTOMA *how to respect Treaties*

A contemporary cartoonist's view of the action at Navarino Bay, the last naval battle fought wholly under sail

epitomised all the arrogant self-assurance of the mid-Victorian John Bull, who could look out from the prosperous safety and security of his island-home on to a world of other nations markedly inferior to his own with, as Palmerston said in private, some 'half-civilised governments', such as those of China, Portugal, and Spanish America, who 'must not only see the Stick but actually feel it on their Shoulders before they yield to that only argument which to them brings conviction'. Any insult to the flag, any hindrance of British trade, any military move, however distant, which might be inimical to British interests was enough to arouse his wrath. The navy was his chosen instrument of terror. Palmerston brought gunboat diplomacy to a fine art and the ships of the Royal Navy sailed the oceans of the world, with their 32 pounder, muzzle-loading guns protruding menacingly through the portholes, ready and willing to avenge any insult. The British middle classes, at the height of their prosperity, prestige, and power loved it – and Palmerston, and the cartoonists, for personifying their own self-righteous supremacy.

During this period, scarcely a single year went by without the ports of some recalcitrant weaker state being blockaded or bombarded. To limit the ambitions of the Egyptian adventurer, Mehemet Ali, who had been nibbling away at

Turkish possessions in the Midde East, the navy bombarded Acre, just north of Haifa, on 30 November 1840, scoring a direct hit on the main magazine which blew much of the port to smithereens and over 1,000 people into eternity. Shortly afterwards, Mehemet Ali gave up his conquests in Palestine and Syria. Meanwhile, on the other side of the world, naval ships were engaged in a far more protracted punishment of China, which, in an attempt to end the drug trade in their own country, had had the audacity to seize a British merchant's cargo of opium in Canton. This insult to the flag and the threat to such a profitable British trade could not go unchallenged and a squadron of ships was fitted out in India to reinforce the two small British naval vessels in the area.

The Chinese Emperor, the proud ruler of his own celestial kingdom, was not immediately impressed and his mandarins returned a letter of protest sent by Lord Palmerston on the ground that it was insulting. With the spirit which helped to give the navy its worldwide reputation for courageous audacity, the captain of a British frigate silenced the guns at Amoy and went ashore to leave a copy of the letter pinned to the beach by a bamboo stake. After further protracted negotiations, and numerous acts of treachery and insult by the Chinese, the British, without too much reluctance, were forced to get out the big stick. Canton and other ports were bombarded; Hongkong was seized; and eventually by the Treaty of Nanking of 1842 the Chinese were forced to open five ports to British trade, to pay an indemnity of twenty-one million dollars, and to cede Hongkong to the British.

By this time there had been a complete change in the caricaturist's world. The invention of the powerful, steam-driven printing press made it possible to print a greater number of copies of a magazine or a newspaper much more quickly, and also to obtain satisfactory reproductions of illustrations and caricatures from hand-engraved wooden blocks. The artist drew the caricature straight on to the block of hard, grainless boxwood, or on paper which was pasted on to the block, which was then handed over to a wood engraver who, with his fantastic skills, could cut out all the white lines and spaces for a full-page magazine cartoon in twenty-four hours. These technical developments made it possible to produce cheaper illustrated periodicals, for which the Victorians had such an insatiable appetite that Charles Knight's *Penny Magazine*, first published in 1832, had a circulation at one time of 180,000 copies a week.

In 1830, Thomas McLean began to publish his *Monthly Sheet of Caricatures* with lithographs by Robert Seymour, who drew in the Gillray tradition, and later by John Doyle, the father of the *Punch* artist, Richard Doyle. This publication, more than any other, helped to destroy the old individualistic relationship between the freelance caricaturist and the London print seller. The etched print, specially produced for the occasion, the hired portfolio, and the single purchased print were increasingly replaced by regular weekly or monthly publications with numerous wood engravings or lithographs. Most of the new satirical and humorous magazines, such as *Figaro in London*, did not last for long, but *Punch*, which was born on 17 July 1841, in the middle of the Opium War, went on from strength to strength to become the leading Victorian humorous magazine, in spite of more serious challenges later from *Fun*, which lasted from 1861 to 1901, *Judy* (1867–1907), and *Moonshine* (1879–1902). It commanded the services of most of the great Victorian cartoonists, including John Leech, Richard Doyle, Charles Keene, and John Tenniel, the first cartoonist to be knighted. After its radical overtures, *Punch* became increasingly conservative in its attitude to domestic affairs, faithfully reflecting the views of the Victorian middle classes and even more of those people who wished to join them. But, in its dislike of ideology and its own capricious inconsistency, its intense patriotism, its ambiguous attitude to the officer class, its support of the common soldier, its unceasing attacks on corruption and incompetence in high places, it remained in the great independent tradition of the Georgian caricaturists.

Right from the start, *Punch* sprang to the defence of its own country with a bellicose contempt for all foreigners which exceeded that of many Georgian caricaturists. In its view, China was then the 'paper tiger'. Its new fortifications in Peking were built of 'japanned canvas and bamboo rods', the guns of blue and white porcelain, and the cannon balls were carved from ivory. The household troops of the Emperor were equipped with 'varnished bladders, containing peas and date stones, which produced a terrific sound upon the least motion'. When *Punch* discovered that 'junk' meant not only a Chinese warship – a 'gimcrack attempt at a vessel' made of the same material as British hat boxes – but also, in naval slang, the salted meat which was Jack Tar's staple fare, it made great play of this in words and pictures. A silhouette entitled *True British Courage* shows some brave sailors dashing into the galley to tackle their tough task of dealing with steaming hot 'junk', which was far more formidable than taking on the Chinese variety. An even more obvious pun, for which *Punch* was renowned, was

The 'Punch' Cartoonists

of his time drawing caricatures of his teachers and of his fellow-students. At the age of eighteen, he published his first work, *Etchings and Sketches* by *A Pen.*

His first drawing in *Punch* appeared in the fourth issue. In all, he contributed over 3,000 drawings, including 600 full-page cartoons. Leech also worked for *Once a Week* and the *Illustrated London News.* In addition, he produced nearly a thousand drawings to illustrate the sporting novels of Surtees and countless other book illustrations, including those for Dickens's *Christmas Books.* Leech took the whole of early Victorian society for his canvas, gently mocking the drunkenness of cabbies, the ruthlessness of ambitious 'mammas', and the mishaps of the hunting field. More than any other artist he gave *Punch* the gentlemanly tone which had such a great appeal for the rising middle classes.

Worn out by incessant work, and a heart condition, Leech died at the age of forty-seven. He was buried in Kensal Green cemetery, near his friend Thackeray, who had died in the previous year.

John Leech (1817–1864), one of the leading artists in *Punch* from its inception in 1841, did a great deal to establish the tone and attitudes of the magazine. His father, who owned the London Coffee House on Ludgate Hill, sent him to Charterhouse, where he met Thackeray, who also became a contributor to *Punch,* and a lifelong friend. Leech studied medicine, but spent much

Richard Doyle (1824–1883) was the second son of an eminent caricaturist, John Doyle, whose lithographs of politicians were extremely popular in the 1830s. Richard, who was born in London, had a precocious talent which was encouraged by his father, and he produced early evidence of his liking for the fantastic and the medieval when he published *The Eglington Tournament* or *The Days of Chivalry Revived* at the age of fifteen. He became a regular contributor to *Punch* at the age of nineteen and designed the cover with its swirling border of elves and fairies which was used for more than a century. His most famous series for the magazine was *Manners and Customs of ye Englyshe.*

Doyle, a Roman Catholic, severed his connection with *Punch* because of its attacks on the Pope and Cardinal Wiseman in 1850. Thereafter, he devoted himself mainly to illustrating books, including Thackeray's *The Newcomes* and *Rebecca and Rowena.* He maintained his interest in the fantastic world of fairies to the end of his life, exhibiting his water colours regularly in the Grosvenor Gallery, where a retrospective exhibition of his work was held two years after his death.

Sir John Tenniel

(1820–1914) did more than any other artist to make *Punch* a national institution. He was born in London and studied at the Royal Academy schools, selling his first painting at the Society of British Artists' exhibition at the age of sixteen and exhibiting at the Royal Academy in the following year. At the age of twenty-five he was commissioned to execute a fresco for the House of Lords. He was also doing book illustrations, and those for Aesop's *Fables* attracted such great critical acclaim that Mark Lemon, the editor of *Punch,* invited Tenniel to succeed Richard Doyle, who had resigned in 1850.

Tenniel became chief cartoonist after Leech died in 1864, a post he held until he retired in 1901. He produced more than 2,000 cartoons and many smaller drawings, one of his most famous being *Dropping the Pilot,* which dealt with Bismarck's resignation. In his later years, his cartoons lost some of their credibility, as he continued to draw statesmen as they were when he had first seen them.

He was the first cartoonist to be knighted in 1893. Tenniel also did many book illustrations, including those for *Alice in Wonderland,* 1865, and *Through the Looking Glass,* 1872, on which his reputation now mainly rests.

Edward Linley Sambourne

(1844–1910) was a *Punch* discovery and creation. Born in London, he was apprenticed to a marine engineering works at Greenwich, where he amused himself by drawing caricatures. The father of a fellow-apprentice showed one of his works to Mark Lemon, the editor of *Punch,* who encouraged Sambourne to do some drawings for the magazine. His first work appeared in *Punch* in 1867, beginning an association which lasted for forty-three years. When Tenniel retired in 1901, Sambourne succeeded him as chief cartoonist. He also illustrated many books including Kingsley's *Water Babies* and Andersen's *Fairy Tales.*

based on 'the illustrious John' the head of the family, repeating the 'celebrated pranks of the Bull in the China shop' with an explanatory silhouette of smashed crockery in case some of its more obtuse readers didn't get the point. The cartoon which was used to illustrate

IMPORTANT NEWS FROM CHINA
Arrival of the Overland Mail!

shows a cheerful-looking sailor with his fingers splayed derisively to his nose, carrying a prostrate Chinese male on his broad back. And so it went on! *Punch* was 'in ecstasies' about the Treaty of Nanking and the 'very pretty pickings' that Britain might secure now that the ports had been opened, though it noted wryly that the indemnity would not come out of the pockets of the bankrupt Chinese, but out of the pockets of British consumers as the Chinese would be forced to increase the tax on their main export of tea. To emphasise the point, it used a small silhouette, entitled *Subtraction*, showing a man picking a neighbour's pocket and transferring the proceeds to the pocket of another man.

Punch had the traditional British reverence for the sailor, who was never any threat to civil liberties, but always the first line of defence against aggressive or impudent foreigners. The laying up of warships in times of peace and the filling of them with crews of impressed seamen in times of war was the perfect way of getting defence on the cheap, so that jolly Jack Tar always had a good public image. Civilians were only too happy to cheer from the shore as the warships sailed off to defend them. The popular image of the sailor, which has scarcely changed since Georgian times, was created mainly by the cartoonists, who portrayed Jack as a jovial lover of fun and escapades, with a ready wit, and a roving eye for the girls. In a caricature called *An Enquiry after Strechit in Gloucestershire*, Woodward shows a young woman on horseback asking a sailor:

> – Pray sir – is this the way to Stretch it?
> – Shiver my top-sails, my lass, if I know a better way.

Although such an uninhibited pun could never have been published in the Victorian *Punch*, which had banned anything even faintly improper from its first issue, its general attitudes to sailors was scarcely any different from those of earlier caricaturists. Jack Tar always talked in a language of his own, full of nautical terms and metaphors, and was much given to wondrous tales of strange events in foreign parts, which he almost alone had seen; of crabs, for instance, which were so huge and powerful that they could drag a cutter after them as if it were 'a mouldy biscuit'. The sailor was credited

IMPORTANT NEWS FROM CHINA.
ARRIVAL OF THE OVERLAND MAIL !

A punning *Punch* cartoon of 1841

with a girl in every port, even though his right to foreign shore leave depended on the whim of his captain and was not made unconditional until 1890; but his sentimental attachment to 'pretty Poll' back home or natural disinclination sometimes enabled him to resist foreign blandishments as we can see in *Jack's Fidelity*. In his home port, Jack was always a big spender, and a heavy drinker, especially if he had prize money to burn. Although, with his great love of free speech, he could sometimes be disrespectful of authority, he remained loyal to his mess mates and his country, and a staunch defender of its liberty. His pride in British freedom was just as great in Victorian times as it had been during the Napoleonic wars, when a caricature by Woodward, engraved

A George Cruikshank illustration to one of Charles Dibdin's songs, published in book form in 1841. A couplet of the song ran:
'You, Miss Copperskin, just
  hold your jaw –
I've sworn to be constant
  to Poll'

JACK'S FIDELITY.

49

by Cruikshank, shows a 'British Tar' reproving a thin, foppish Frenchman who has come to Britain to teach the people the true meaning of liberty with the words:

A lath like you – teach Britons to be free!
Damme – we learn it with our ABC.

The stock image of the sailor was sustained and further enhanced by Charles Dibdin, who voiced the same kind of sentiments as those expressed in caricatures and cartoons. Born near Southampton in 1745, he began to give one-man performances of his own sea-songs in 1788, which brought him fame, though not fortune, during the Napoleonic wars, when patriotic audiences flocked to his shows just as eagerly as they crowded round printsellers' windows to see the caricatures celebrating Nelson's latest victory. Dibdin's most famous song was *Tom Bowling*, but he wrote about a hundred others including *'Twas in the good ship Rover, Grog and the Girls, Britons United,* and *A Plague of those Musty Old Lubbers.* When a collection of his songs was published in 1841 with illustrations by George Cruikshank, it became an instant best-seller with the Queen buying fifty copies and the Admiralty ten times as many. The sentimental regard for the sailor was given fashionable recognition when many little middle-class children were forced to wear sailor suits in late Victorian and Edwardian times.

It was on this jolly image that the general public chose to concentrate, ignoring the less palatable truths which also appeared in the early caricatures, where 'Poor Jack' is almost as common a figure as his *alter ego* 'Jolly Jack'. One of the longest-standing complaints of seamen was over the arbitrary operations of press gangs, used for centuries to fill ships in times of war, which was an inevitable consequence of the civilian reluctance to pay the proper price for its defence. Merchant seamen were sometimes seized and pressed into service before their ship had docked; and even if they escaped their fate, they could still be picked up by a gang of tough sailors and local bullies, armed with cudgels, who roamed the ports looking for any man who could possibly be mistaken for a sailor. With its brutal violence, its great expense, and its doubtful legality, the press gang had long been one of the main targets of the caricaturists' abuse from Gillray's ironically-titled *The Liberty of the Subject* of 1779 to Henry Heath's *The British Press,* published nearly fifty years later in 1824. By that time the terrible poverty and starvation at home which was a consequence of the Napoleonic wars had allowed the greatly reduced number of warships to be manned almost entirely by volunteers and

Henry Heath's punning
cartoon of 1824

boy-entrants; but to provide a larger number of recruits, the
Admiralty introduced regular long-term engagements for
sailors in 1853, a timely innovation coinciding, as it did, with
the outbreak of the Crimean War.

The need to maintain discipline among the miserable
crowd of recruits that the press gang usually provided,
described variously by naval captains as 'blackguards', 'ragg
tagg', and 'sorry poor creatures that don't earn half the
victuals they eat', resulted in the liberal use of the cat-o'-
nine-tails in naval vessels, which helped to deter the better
class of merchant seaman from volunteering for service.
According to one rating, John Nicol, naval floggings also
horrified the Chinese, whom Palmerston was later to
describe as 'half-civilised', for he saw them 'weep like
children' for some British sailors who were flogged in a
Chinese port and heard them say: 'Hey, yaw. Englishman
too much cruel – too much flog – too much flog'. It is
doubtful if there was much knowledge outside the Admiralty
and naval ports of how frequently the lash was used. There
appear to be no cartoons on the subject apart from George

Cruikshank's well-known illustration to a tale by an 'Old Sailor' whose purpose was to praise the loyalty of shipmates not to condemn the barbaric nature of the punishment. In fact, it was not primarily the lash which made British sailors fight so bravely but the desire to achieve a victory for, as one member of the lower deck said, it was only victory which could give them the chance to return home to their wife and family again. Flogging was never officially abolished in the navy, only suspended, though its use declined dramatically after annual returns had to be submitted to Parliament from 1853. The last naval flogging took place in 1880, a year before it was officially abolished in the army.

But the evidence of the other price that many sailors had to pay for their service to the nation was a common sight in all the big cities and the ports – and in the cartoons – as veterans of some remote conflict limped along the streets on their wooden legs or tried to grasp a pint pot with their hooked arm. They were left to suffer, often unaided and pensionless. Although a Royal Hospital had been founded at Greenwich in 1695 to care for the poor, the old, and the wounded, it could not cope with all those who needed its protection, and many sailors were left to beg or to perish in the street, just as, earlier, after the defeat of the Armada, victorious sailors had

Above: George Cruikshank's version of a naval flogging. A shipmate confesses at the last moment that he is the guilty man

to roam the streets of Margate in search of shelter and to die of their wounds or disease – 'a most pitiful sight', as their commander, Charles Howard, complained to Queen Elizabeth's chief minister. This continuing ingratitude to the men who had given the nation such great service aroused the sympathy of the infant *Punch*, which published a cartoon of one of the many 'Poor Jacks' in London who carried his two-year-old daughter strapped in a box on his back as he tramped the streets with hat outstretched. In 1830 William Heath had drawn even more radical conclusions from the wounded ex-serviceman's plight in his caricature of *The Civil List!!!* A year later small pensions were granted to sailors with twenty-one years' service, and from 1853 they were given to all men on long-term engagements so that the Royal Hospital was closed in 1869. But low basic rates of pay continued to remain a source of grievance. As has been seen, the admiralty had never been very generous paymasters. It was not until sailors mutinied at Spithead in 1797 that they were given a pay rise of about twenty-three per cent, the first for nearly 150 years.

The Admiralty was scarcely more generous to its officers. With the savage retrenchment after the Napoleonic wars, there were far too many of them chasing too few ships so that

Below: William Heath draws a radical contrast between the Chelsea pensioner, a starving farm labourer, and a penniless sailor, and the happy band of aristocratic ladies who benefit from the large Civil List pensions which stream out of the Red Book – a symbol of Old Corruption

THE CIVIL LIST !!!

by 1825, ninety per cent of all officers were unemployed. They could not be sacked as they held permanent commissions and there was no provision for retirement. Instead they were given what was euphemistically called half-pay, though this could be as little as twenty per cent of their regular salary with no chance of supplementing it by the perk of prize money. Promotion was so slow that by 1840 one lieutenant had held the same rank for sixty years and another officer had been a commander for nearly fifty years. Above the rank of captain, promotion went by seniority, and it was blocked by admirals of seventy years or more of age, decrepit survivors from the Napoleonic wars, who were totally unfit for further service. It was not until 1870 that any officer could be placed on the retired list when he was past his peak.

The navy remained a small, self-contained world with its own distinctive attitudes, standards, and ambitions which civilians applauded but did not have to share. Its men sailed across all the oceans of the world and fought many battles for small rewards and with few hopes except as Woodward put it in *The Sailor's Prayer* for 'a stout ship, honest messmates, plenty of grog, a good commander, a good prize, brandy and tobacco'. It is little wonder that these simple men, who have provided the main bulwark of British independence and freedom throughout the centuries, should have always claimed such a large measure of affection from the public who paid them such a pittance for their great service. Despite the caricaturists' exposure of the great cruelties, hardships, and discomforts inherent in the naval life of those times, the public remained largely indifferent to these views. For them, the navy was a symbol of British power and supremacy; they did not want to probe too deeply into the finer details of reality, or the means by which power was achieved. They concentrated on the great victories, the audacity, and the courage, on 'Jolly Jack' and not on 'Poor Jack', who limped his solitary way through city streets and the cartoons. The cartoonist's power to influence public opinion was often blunted in this way by a consensus of public indifference.

3

HEROISM
AND
HUMILIATION

A TRUMP CARD (IGAN).

The Crimean War demonstrated only too clearly, and humiliatingly, to the great British public that, however terrifying the Royal Navy might be to 'semi-civilised' nations like the Chinese, and however successful the British army might be in defeating native Indian, Burmese, or Maori forces, neither was equipped to fight a war against a major European power like Russia, even though in British eyes it was scarcely more civilised than China.

Punch was by that time at the height of its influence, possessing a virtual monopoly in the cartoon world, which was not to be seriously challenged until 1861 when *Fun* started publication. Its cartoons reflected the feelings of the middle classes to the near-disastrous war: their exasperation at the muddle which offended all their pride in British efficiency in the civilian sphere; their antagonism to the surviving members of the unreformed aristocratic establishment who still held a dominant position in political councils of war; their hostility to the ancient, incompetent military and naval commanders, who had still not been ousted from power. *Punch*'s savage humour and unceasing attacks were major factors in bringing about the fall of the Prime Minister, Aberdeen, and were also instrumental in the institution of some minor military reforms, though it was not until the Liberals came to power in 1868 that the first full-scale attempts at thorough reform of the army were made.

The Crimean War was the only major European conflict in which Britain was engaged between the end of the Napoleonic war and the outbreak of the First World War. It was caused mainly by the aggressive designs of the Tsar, Nicholas I, on the weakening Turkish empire. War broke out between Turkey and Russia in September 1853, after the Tsar had claimed the right to protect Christians in the Ottoman empire. At first, there had been little British enthusiasm to be implicated in this 'absurd' quarrel which, as *Punch* wrote, 'would have long ago been brought to a conclusion, by being overwhelmed with a storm of ridicule', if it had involved individuals and not nations. 'Drat the Eastern Question,' said *Punch* in November 1853, a sentiment which has been re-echoed by succeeding generations of schoolchildren as they labour through their history examinations. But, as it became increasingly evident that the Russian bear needed to have its 'nails cut', a wave of self-righteous indignation swept through the nation and the pages of *Punch*. Those people who didn't want to join the righteous fight were reviled and castigated. The leaders of the Peace Society, Richard Cobden and John Bright, who

Previous page: John Leech's view of the Charge of the Light Brigade led by Lord Cardigan

Left: General Brown, commander of the Light Division, with his staff during the Crimean War

had once been the heroes of the middle classes in their efforts to repeal the Corn Laws, were now branded as traitors. There was no respect either for those selfish men who put their own petty interests before those of their country. *Punch*, which had always had a certain streak of anti-Semitism in Victorian times even though its long serving editor, Mark Lemon, was of Jewish extraction, published a cartoon just before the outbreak of the war showing a recruiting sergeant appealing to a 'swell' Jewish lawyer, with long hair and sideburns, to serve the Queen. 'Much rayther remain as I am,' he coolly replies, 'and serve de Queen's Bench.' Much more to *Punch's* liking was the patriotic sailor, stripped to the waist, with a tattooed anchor on one arm and 'Poll' on the other, who is offering to 'salute the Rooshians' in the most appropriate way, as he crouches down to pick up another heavy shot for his gun, while in the background the dismembered Russian eagle is being blown sky-high among swirling clouds of smoke. By the time Britain and France had declared war on Russia on 27 March 1854, the jingoistic propaganda had done its work. There was an absolute moral certainty in the justice of Britannia's cause and in the enduring strength and valour of the British lion. It was simply a question of *Right against Wrong*.

Once the war had started, the British public – and *Punch* – thirsted for action, but it took nearly ten weeks before an expeditionary force of some 18,000 British troops under Lord Raglan was finally disembarked at Gallipoli; and then, deciding that their presence there was useless and unnecessary, the high command had them shipped, some in convict hulks which had been purloined as troop transports, to Varna in Bulgaria, about 480 kilometres to the north. Disgusted by these delays, *Punch* depicted the Duke of Cambridge, who had just been promoted major-general, riding off from Paris for a leisurely sight-seeing tour to Vienna, while the guns pointed the other way. It complained peevishly that 'the most important military movements that have as yet taken place have been principally those which have been accomplished by the energy and activity of distinguished officers, figuring in the "Lancers".'

By August 1854, cholera, which was to claim many more British lives than Russian bullets, had gained its first victory at Varna. Undeterred, the allied generals decided to continue with their plan of invading the Crimea and of capturing the main seaport of Sebastopol, even though they had little intelligence of Russian strength apart from off-shore observation. Early in September, the allied fleet set sail, with the decks and holds of the French warships so crammed with soldiers that it would have been impossible for the ships' guns to have been fired. It was mainly the fine weather and Russian caution which allowed some 30,000 British troops and about the same number of French to land unharmed at Eupatoria, even though the invasion fleet had anchored in mid-passage while the allied commanders quarrelled about the landing beach, and the Crimean coast was hastily reconnoitred to find a different one from that which had originally been selected.

The war on land began far more auspiciously than it continued. Within six days of the unopposed landings, the allied armies, including the Welch Fusiliers, the Guards, and the Black Watch, had driven the Russian troops off the heights above the Alma river by successive bayonet charges against the enemy's gun emplacements. This victory delighted *Punch*, which published a cartoon showing somewhat prematurely the *Bursting of the Russian Bubble* and another of British, French, and Turkish soldiers hoisting their colours in triumph. The Allies, however, failed to take advantage of their victory by marching on Sebastopol and instead started to dig in and to construct siege batteries. There was little sense of urgency or co-operation between the Services. When the Royal Navy started to attack Russian positions with long-range bombardments, Lord Raglan asked them to desist as he thought that it might disquiet the army!

The main Allied supply base and headquarters in the Crimea was Balaklava, a small seaport some 13 kilometres south-east of Sebastopol. On 25 October 1854, a Russian force of about 12,000 men tried to seize the base, but they were repulsed by a Highland regiment and the brilliant charge of the Heavy Brigade under General Scarlett. But it was not that success which was remembered from the battle. With the unique British capacity, which always astonishes foreigners, to turn a defeat into victory if only it is heroic and foolhardy enough, the nation exulted, as it has done ever since, in the disastrous Charge of the Light Brigade commanded by Lord Cardigan, which owing to a misunderstanding of orders, was ordered to charge up a long valley against the full force of the Russian guns. Of the 673 men who took part nearly a third were killed or wounded. *Punch* could scarcely contain its delight. It published a cartoon showing *paterfamilias* brandishing a poker from the hearth, as he delightedly reads the report of the 'grand charge' in his newspapers, while the other members of his numerous brood all shout and cheer, apart from the eldest daughter – and his wife – who cannot keep back their tears for the brave, fallen heroes. But *Punch*, no respecter of even the greatest hero who committed some subsequent misdemeanour, was fickle in its affections. When Lord Cardigan resigned his command after the battle of Inkerman on 5 November when no cavalry was engaged, and returned to England where he was received several times by the Queen, *Punch* was quite indignant and suggested respectfully that when he dined with her again, the Queen might suggest that his resignation was not exactly the thing to encourage devotion in other soldiers.

After these three great victories within seven weeks, the reports from the eastern front became increasingly gloomy. The troops dug in for the long siege of Sebastopol in the bitter winter which had started with a violent storm nine days after the battle of Inkerman. There was appalling inactivity, incompetence, and muddle. The narrow track between Balaklava and the trenches near Sebastopol became completely blocked at times by mud and snow, while supplies lay rotting in the harbour; the troops lacked clothes,

HOW TO GET RID OF AN OLD WOMAN.

Punch's proposal for the future employment of the ineffectual Prime Minister, Lord Aberdeen. Shortly afterwards, he resigned following a vote of censure in Parliament

equipment, food, and medical supplies so that many of them perished from hunger, frost, and fever.

Punch could not contain its anger and launched a series of bitter attacks, which continued almost to the end of the war, on the incompetent old men of privileged birth in high places who were responsible for these disasters. The Prime Minister, the Earl of Aberdeen, who was in his seventieth year, was repeatedly castigated for his weakness, lethargy, and lack of resolution. *Punch* suggested that the best way to get rid of an old woman like him would be to send him off with the nurses to the eastern front. When he resigned and was succeeded in February 1855, by that equally old but still dynamic and pugnacious warrior, Lord Palmerston, *Punch* was delighted. It published a cartoon showing Palmerston, equipped with shovel and besom, preparing to clear up the 'Dirty Doorstep' of No. 10 Downing Street, which was littered with blunders, routine, precedent, incapacity, delay, twaddle, and disorder. In its attacks on ancient, blundering politicians of the old school, *Punch* was faithfully reflecting the antagonism of its readership to the aristocratic establishment which had excluded the middle classes from power for so many decades before the passing of the First Reform Act of 1832. Their attitudes towards the military establishment were even more hostile, as the armed forces still remained bastions of aristocratic power from which the middle classes were almost entirely excluded.

But politicians were easier to remove than the ancient commanders, veterans of the Napoleonic wars, who clung obstinately to the positions of authority which they had waited so long to inherit. Viscount Hardinge, who had succeeded Wellington as commander-in-chief of the army in 1852, at the age of sixty-seven, was in *Punch's* eyes another old woman – or 'lady' – who was only fit to be 'Chief Pensioner of Chelsea Hospital'. The commander-in-chief in the Crimea, Lord Raglan, who had a penchant for wearing civilian clothes and peculiar bonnets, was yet another veteran of the Napoleonic wars, and had served on Wellington's staff in the Peninsula. Although he had lost an arm at Waterloo, he had never commanded even a battalion in the field before he took charge of the operations in the Crimea. His despatches from the front were concerned mainly with the weather, probably, *Punch* thought, because 'he is adapting his style to the taste of his countrymen, who are always talking about the weather when they have nothing else to talk about'. A couple of months after Palmerston had come to office, he ordered a Day of Fast and Humiliation for the losses sustained by the troops in the Crimea, which

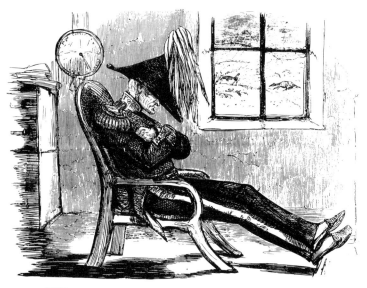

THE GENERAL FAST (ASLEEP). HUMILIATING—VERY !

The savage attack on
Lord Raglan published
on 24 March 1855

Punch, with some intricate word play turned into an attack on Raglan in its cartoon *The General Fast (Asleep). Humiliating – Very!* These opinions of Raglan were shared not only by the middle classes at home but also by many of the men in the trenches. A letter written by Private E. Griffiths from the 'camp before Sevastopol', which is preserved in the National Army Museum, describes Raglan as 'old and foolish, not fit for this service'. It was little wonder that with such a weak inactive commander, the troops should have become completely demoralised. Worn out by constant public criticisms, and suffering from dysentry which was to kill so many of his troops, Raglan died on 3 July 1855, at the age of sixty-six, less than a year after he had been made field marshal. He was succeeded by yet another veteran of the Peninsular Wars, General Simpson who was, however, only sixty-two.

The Royal Navy was in the hands of old men, too. At the beginning of the war, the commander-in-chief in the Black Sea, Vice-Admiral Dundas, was sixty-nine. He had waited as a post captain for thirty-four years for promotion to flag rank. In December 1854, he was succeeded by Rear-Admiral Sir Edmund Lyons, who was a mere sixty-four years of age; the commander-in-chief in the Baltic, Sir Charles Napier, was sixty-eight. It was little wonder that with such ancient and often decrepit veterans in command the navy should have played such an ineffectual role in the war, contenting itself mainly with distant bombardments of the shores in the Crimea and in the Baltic, which started numerous forest fires in Finland – then an autonomous region of Russia – including one which destroyed a valuable consignment of pitch that had already been bought by the British government and was only awaiting shipment. Earlier, the Baltic fleet had captured the Russian fortress of Bomarsund on the Aland Islands north-east of Stockholm, but this remote victory had no influence on the outcome of the war. The navy's activities in the Black Sea were almost as inconclusive. There were no great battles or assaults, though many troop transports were lost not through enemy action but through storms.

The war revealed how far Britain had allowed its first line of defence to rot. There were not enough steam and screw-propelled vessels, partly through parliamentary-enforced retrenchment, but also because many men in high command still lived nostalgically in the age of sail and resented their spotless, holystoned decks being smeared with smuts from the funnels of these new steam engines, which had only been introduced thirty years before. The flagship in the Black Sea, the *Britannia*, was a sailing vessel which was towed by steam tugs. There were no heavy-rifled guns and no armoured ships, which the French had been advocating since 1842 and which they actually introduced into service before the British with the launching of the world's first ironclad, *Gloire*, in 1859.

This lethargy, muddle, and incompetence was, unfortunately, not restricted to commanders in the field or at sea, but was even more apparent and harmful in the transport, commissariat, and medical departments. Coffee beans were sent out to the Crimea, green and unroasted, and the Christmas puddings were so hard that *Punch* feared that they might be 'fired away under the idea that they were round shot'. Soldiers' wives – and *Punch* – were always complaining about the slow delivery of letters and newspapers to the 'gallant fellows' in the East, who had much more to fear from their own generals than they ever had to take from the Russians. Many of the woollen drawers sent out in the first bitter winter of the campaign had been made to fit boys of seven to ten years of age. If this, commented *Punch*, was 'deliberate fraud', it was not only 'murder, and wholesale murder, but it is murder double blackened by treason to the state' for which the sentence should be hanging; if it was only 'gross negligence', the punishment might be merely 'transportation for life'. There was no doubt about the heinous guilt of a Mr Sturgeon who had earlier deliberately supplied horses in the Crimea with rotten hay: wet and mixed with dirt and shavings. *Punch* published a 'fancy portrait' of him crawling abjectly on the ground with a fish's body appropriate to his name.

Many attacks were made by *Punch* on the incompetent old men who ran the medical department of the army, the commissariat, and the main military hospital at Scutari in Turkey. Dr Andrew Smith, chief of the Army Medical Department in St James's Place, was suffering from 'general paralysis of the active powers, which has gradually been growing upon him during forty years service' which was accompanied 'by a total loss of the faculty of hearing reason'. Dr Menzies, who was in charge at Scutari, was 'utterly unfit' for his duties and was so occupied with writing at his desk for ten or twelve hours a day that he could not spare the time to inspect the wards except on one or two occasions and even then he was 'entirely incapable of exerting the senses of sight, speech or smell'. The men in command of the commissariat presented an even more 'melancholy spectacle'. They were 'almost all advanced in life, and equally feeble in mind and body; and it is obvious at a glance that to impose the task of feeding the Army on men unable to feed themselves. . .was a cruel mockery.' When the Queen paid a visit to the invalids of the Crimea, *Punch* took the opportunity to imagine what she would have found if she had visited these 'Imbeciles of the Crimea' instead.

Below: The *Punch* cartoon published on 14 April 1855 showing the Queen visiting the 'Imbeciles of the Crimea'

THE QUEEN VISITING THE IMBECILES OF THE CRIMEA.

"WELL, JACK! HERE'S GOOD NEWS FROM HOME. WE'RE TO HAVE A MEDAL."
"THAT'S VERY KIND. MAYBE ONE OF THESE DAYS WE'LL HAVE A COAT TO STICK IT ON?"

Above: The Crimean War created a new style of humour in *Punch*, which was much more sympathetic to the common soldier

Some of the victims of this incompetence and muddle – the ragged, starving, freezing, sick troops on the ground, complained bitterly about their fate of being left to rot leaderless, unoccupied, and isolated in the snow and mud of the Crimea. Private T. Hagger, of the 23rd Royal Welch Fusiliers, wrote to his parents on 1 December 1854: 'The people at home think that the troops out here are well provided for. I am sorry to say that they are treated worse than dogs at home.' But their plight was neither as unknown nor as neglected as he believed. For almost the first time, the British public was made aware by the *Punch* cartoons and the despatches of that great war correspondent, William Howard Russell, in *The Times* of how much the British soldier suffered, and had always suffered, on behalf of the civilians who remained in safety and security at home. Although the troops complained, quite justly, they retained the ability to laugh at their misfortune. They were sustained not by their lethargic generals or the bungling commissariat, but by their own native sense of stoical fortitude and the ironic sense of humour which has always been the distinguishing mark of the British soldier. A cartoon of two ragged campaigners discussing the issue of a campaign medal, which was published in *Punch* on 17 February 1855, encapsulates just the same kind of 'Old Bill' spirit which was to be exploited so effectively by Bruce Bairnsfather some sixty years later during the First World War.

Punch had enormous sympathy and admiration for its 'gallant fellows' in the East. At the beginning of the war, the troops were still forced to fight in full-dress uniform, which was entirely unsuitable for campaigning in the Crimea. Their long-skirted coats were so close fitting that, in *Punch's* words, there were 'sad accounts from the seat of war of gaunt guardsmen fainting under the effects of tight lacing'. They were also forced to wear a leather stock around their necks, or a black choker as it was more popularly known. Although it was desirable that soldiers should 'never bend the neck or bow the head to the enemy', said *Punch*, 'it is a pity that apoplexy or suffocation should be the occasional price of his erect attitude'. Partly as a result of this ridicule, the tight coat was abandoned in favour of a more serviceable, looser tunic, similar to those worn by the French; and the tall, cylindrical head-dress, known as the 'Albert' shako, which had reputedly been introduced by the Prince Consort, was replaced by a smaller French-style kepi, though *Punch* did not like the latter any better. In fact, there was an increasing informality of dress during the Crimean campaign, as junior officers in particular made or obtained from home any article of clothing which would help to keep out the bitter cold. Cardigans, named after Lord Cardigan, and Balaklava helmets, were among the products of British improvisation;

Right: The original caption to this *Punch* cartoon read: 'Here! Hi! Bill! C-C-C-C-Catch hold o' my musket! My head's C-C-C-Coming off!'

Below: Contrasting views of hardships in the Crimea, published by *Punch* in 1856

Highland Officer in the Crimea, according to the Romantic Ideas of Sentimental Young Ladies.

Ditto, according to the Actual Fact.

THE BLACK CHOKER.
Dedicated to the Powers that Be.

Jones: "HERE! HI! BILL!! C-C-C-CATCH HOLD O' MY MUSKET! MY HEAD'S C-C-COMING"

but it was not until the early months of 1855 that Highland regiments were officially allowed to replace the kilt with warm tartan trousers. By the time the war had ended, some Highland officers in the Crimea were more practically dressed than their romantic lady friends at home realised.

When the ordinary British soldier – or sailor – was allowed to fight, he proved his worth time after time, just as valiantly as he had ever done in the past. There were many individual acts of great bravery. A sergeant in the Coldstreams, for instance, captured sixteen Russians single-handed; Private Joseph Coulter refused to break ranks but kept on firing even though he had been severely wounded by four Russian bullets and fragments of a shell; while Private Wheatley threw an unexploded shell over the parapet when it fell into the battery where he was stationed. During the Baltic campaign, Mate Charles Davis Lucas flung a live shell overboard after it had fallen on the deck of the *Hecla*. Yet the rewards for similar acts of gallantry were often unequal. Mate Lucas was immediately promoted lieutenant and was later awarded the Victoria Cross, which was instituted during the Crimean War; but Private Wheatley received only a gratuity of £5. *Punch* had unbounded admiration for these brave men with their great courage and devotion to duty, which was matched only by its reverence for the 'tender, gallant' Florence Nightingale, whose name provided such an obvious opportunity for punning pictures

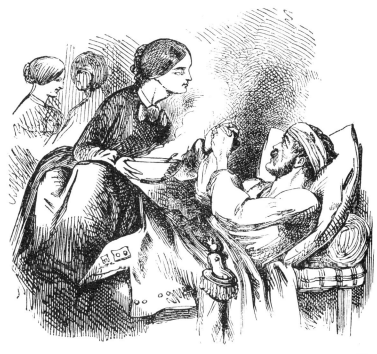

Right: *The Nightingale's Song to the Sick Soldier*, a *Punch* cartoon of 1854

that even *Punch* was occasionally too shamefaced to seize it.

The attitude of *Punch* towards army officers was more ambiguous. Like most civilians, it had little time for the tall, languid officer, with his affected speech and arrogant manner, *The Drawing Room Captain*, 'the hero of a hundred balls', who had been savagely satirised in the magazine almost from the first issue. Cavalry officers were one of the traditional targets of caricaturists' abuse. In the 1820s, the Tenth Hussars, one of the most fashionable light cavalry regiments of which the Prince Regent had been commander-in-chief until his accession, had been mercilessly pilloried by the caricaturists for their lack of social grace and offensive behaviour to civilians and ladies in Dublin, where the ballrooms resounded with their catch phrase, 'Tenth don't dance.' *Punch* kept up the attacks. Cavalry officers invariably sported a moustache in peacetime which was often accompanied by a beard in the time of war. Just before the Crimean War broke out, *Punch* pictured two cavalry officers talking in their mess:

> – Good gracious! Here's a horwible go! The infantwy's going to gwow a moustache!
> – Yaw don't mean that! There's only one alternative for us. WE must shave!!

The same heroic spirit of self-sacrifice continued after hostilities had started. Six months after the outbreak of the war, another cavalry officer, Lieutenant Plunger, complete with carefully curled moustache but as yet beardless, lounges languidly outside his tent in Turkey smoking a cigar. He asks a passing Turkish cavalry officer in his red fez: 'I say, old fellah! Do you think it pwobable the Infantry will accompany us to Sebastopol?'

In Victorian times, and for many years thereafter, the army did not constitute a homogeneous whole but remained a loose confederation of separate and distinctive regiments, or gentlemen's clubs, each with its own rigid traditions which governed all aspects of speech, behaviour, and attitudes. Officers fought not only for their queen and their country, but also, and perhaps more immediately, for the honour of their regiment. It was this concept and their sense of loyalty, their sense of duty, and their unquestioning obedience of orders which enabled them to perform such reckless deeds of courage as the Charge of the Light Brigade. The honour of the regiment had to be preserved not only on the battlefield but also in every aspect, great or small, of daily life, which could sometimes lead to pettish quarrels and schoolboy behaviour in the mess with officers being sent to

Right: The drawing-room captain with his lap dog and languid air was always unpopular with *Punch* – and the mass of the stolid, Victorian middle classes

THE DRAWING-ROOM CAPTAIN.

SHOPPING !

There was some agitation during the Crimean War for the purchase of commissions to be abolished, but the practice was not stopped until 1871

Coventry for some alleged offence. These disputes occasionally swelled into sectarian strife involving every officer in the regiment, so that, in the middle of the war, the Queen was forced to intervene personally in a series of absurd courts-martial, which had started when a lieutenant in the 46th Foot hit a brother officer with a candlestick for allegedly using 'disgusting' language.

Punch was no more pleased by these courts-martial than it was by the tendency of some officers to treat the army as a private club which they could leave or enter as and when they wished. When General Simpson took over command in the Crimea, he granted many officers leave of absence on 'urgent private affairs', even though the war had still not ended. *Punch* published a cartoon showing a long line of soldiers outside the general's tent with their spokesman saying: 'Please, general, may me and these other chaps have leave to go home on urgent *private* affairs?'

This tendency to treat the army as a club was still sustained and perpetuated by the purchase system which restricted commissions and promotions up to the rank of lieutenant-colonel in the Guards, the cavalry, the fusilier corps, the rifle corps, and the regiments of the line to those members of a social élite who could afford to pay the entrance fee. During the Crimean War, the official rate for the rank of lieutenant-colonel ranged from £9,000 in the Foot Guards to £4,500 in a regiment of the line, a very considerable sum of money in those days. A majority in a good regiment cost about £5,000 and a captaincy about £3,500, though these prices were often greatly inflated on the flourishing black market and by the profits and speculations of the numerous agents who traded in army commissions. There was much talk during the war of abolishing the sale of commissions. The system was satirised by *Punch* in a cartoon *Shopping!* but the regiments objected to any change because it might admit officers of an undesirable type and the British taxpayer was also opposed because he would have had to foot the bill for any change. With typical lassitude, the British compromised and did absolutely nothing.

Fortunately the purchase system did not produce only 'drawing room captains', as *Punch* was quick and proud to proclaim. In one cartoon, a tall, thin officer in mufti bending over graciously to ask a society belle to dance, is transformed in the adjoining cut to a brave young man in uniform with sword upraised leading his troops in a charge against the Russian guns. 'Our Guards,' comments *Punch*. 'They can play; and, by jove, they can fight too.' During the battle of Inkerman, the confusion and the lack of strategy in the high command threw all the heavy weight of responsibility on regimental officers. *Punch* could not praise too highly the conduct of Colonel Upton of the Guards Division and all his 'noble young men' who supplied 'a rallying point to the shattered battalions'.

The siege of Sebastopol, whose defences had been strongly reinforced while Lord Raglan was engaged in writing his weather reports, continued for a year from September 1854, to September 1855, when the Russians evacuated the city. 'The enormous disproportion,' commented *Punch*, 'between the number of bomb-shells thrown into Sebastopol by our besieging army, and the damage which has been done to that city, must have astonished everybody.' Some fighting continued in a desultory way, but for all practical purposes the war was over, though peace was not finally declared until March 1856. There were few regrets except among the naval 'lieutenants of 1812'

HARD UPON THE OLD LIEUTENANTS OF 1812, OR THEREABOUTS.

who had been robbed again of all chances of promotion.

At home, there was an equivalent sense of relief that the humiliations of the war had finally ended. The income tax, which had been reintroduced by Sir Robert Peel twelve years before the war broke out, had risen to a rate of over 6 per cent, but with the peace it came down again to its more normal level of just under 3 per cent. There had been the usual profiteering particularly in bread and in sugar after two or three speculators had cornered the markets. There was also an increase in the adulteration of food. *Punch* published a cartoon of a criminal-looking grocer with closely-cropped hair, whose huge sacks of sand, red lead, plaster of paris, and nux vomica were carefully concealed below the counter. An innocent-looking girl in a bonnet is asking:

> If you please, sir, mother says, will you let her have a quarter of a pound of your best tea to kill the rats with, and a ounce of chocolate as would get rid of the black beadles?

Above: A *Punch* cartoon published just after the end of the war. The original caption read: 'Confound the Peace, I say! If we'd had but a slap at 'em this year in the Baltic, I might have got a command – and now I may stick as I am for the next forty years!'

Well-meaning ladies did their bit for the war effort just as they had done during the Napoleonic wars. They lifted up their little well-dressed children so that they could put their penny in the church plate for the less privileged children of the gallant soldiers in the East; they knitted cardigans and Balaklava helmets furiously and ripped up their flannel petticoats to make warm drawers for the soldiers; and they sent out piles of old books and newspapers to the East. These patriotic gestures also prompted some male civilians to make the supreme sacrifice. In one cartoon, a long-haired playwright, sitting by his overflowing waste paper basket, is made to say: 'So they are sending out books to amuse the poor fellows at Scutari – and very proper. I will send them five-and-twenty copies of my last five-act tragedy of *The Roman Grandmother*.' But *Punch* had some laconic advice: 'No! Don't!'

There was a great increase in street violence, as there often is in wartime, with garroters prowling the dark streets and strangling their victims from behind before they robbed them. The fashionable young man who had not gone to war adopted the pose of the 'languid swell', carrying a small lady-like umbrella and wearing large moustaches and mutton-chop whiskers which were allowed to grow later into luxuriant beards, in the hope, expressed by Young Snobley, 'a regular lady-killer', that the girls might think he was 'a horficer just come back from the Crimear'. Women's hats expanded to an enormous size but it was not until just after the war that their skirts gained an equivalent girth when women started to wear the crinoline.

Below: *Punch* kept up its attack on the stupidity of army officers after the war was over. The original caption read: 'The surprise and delight of the general commanding-in-chief at the success of the new straw stables at Aldershot.'

Peace produced just the same reaction as it has done after so many major wars: an immense sense of relief and immediate civilian howls for cuts in defence spending. *Punch*, which had been so bellicose and so very critical of the lack of modern equipment, was no less inconsistent. Only two months after the war had ended it wrote reprovingly: 'Peace is restored, and, therefore, we are launching gun boats and trying new howitzers with remarkable activity.' But, this time, the naval and military high commands were determined not to be caught napping again. The navy, which had started continuous service engagements just before the war, set its seal of approval on the new breed of sailor by introducing a uniform for which the men had pleaded for so long. In the following year, it started to experiment with breech-loading guns and three years later launched the *Warrior*, the first real ironclad in the world with an iron hull and armour plating on the main deck. The army made some administrative reforms by abolishing some of its numerous departments and merging others, and by introducing a breech-loading rifle in 1867; but some of its other innovations, such as the construction of straw-built stables at Aldershot, were not quite as successful, which provided *Punch* with fresh opportunities for cartoon laughter at the army's expense.

Like its middle-class readers, *Punch* had extremely muddled and inconsistent attitudes towards the armed forces. It wanted improvements and reforms so long as they did not involve additional expense. Its sympathy for the common soldier was based just as much on antagonism towards the old guard as it was on liberal sympathies. It could admire arrogant incompetence if it was sufficiently heroic and daring, but could not tolerate it as a general way of life. What *Punch*, and its readers, wanted from the armed forces were the same qualities as it liked to find in civilian life: total assurance, constant success, British supremacy. These needs were to become even more extreme as the Victorian age progressed, bringing its first disturbing evidence that in some spheres Britain was being slowly surpassed by foreign rivals.

4

MUTINY AND THE RAJ

JUSTICE.

There was a completely separate and very different kind of army during the first twenty years of Victoria's reign, which provided the biggest opportunities for middle-class youths, unblessed by personal fortune, to obtain a commission. The Indian army was unique. Formed and controlled by the East India Company, it was a large force of some quarter-of-a-million men, of whom the vast majority until the Indian Mutiny of 1857–8 were sepoys or Indian soldiers, led and strengthened by some 15,000 British officers and men. In contrast to the Queen's army, where all commissions had to be bought, except in the technical branches of the Royal Artillery and the Royal Engineers, commissions in the Indian army were not for sale. They were gained either by attending the company's own college at Addiscombe House in Surrey or through direct entry as a cadet, which was the invariable procedure for the cavalry man for whom no training was deemed to be necessary. After completing their two-year course in England, these young officers, their minds hopefully stuffed full of Hindustani, geology, mathematics, and chemistry and more romantically with exotic visions of the East with its opulent palaces, its bejewelled women, and its strange customs, sailed out on the long, tedious, and often dangerous voyage to India, prepared to die in honour and in glory for their company and their country and to hold back the savage tribesmen of the hills and to defeat the fierce nations of the sub-continent, like the turbaned Sikhs, who were finally conquered after two savage wars in 1845–6 and 1848–9.

The reality, however, was often quite different and initially disillusioning. The newly-commissioned officer was appointed to one of the three presidencies into which the army was divided, the Madras, the Bombay, or the Bengal, popularly known in the cabalistic circles of that distant land where nicknames and transliterations from native language proliferated, as the Mulls from mulligatawny soup, the Ducks from Bombay Duck, and the qui-hyes from *koi-hai*, the command used in Bengal to make a native servant come running. Those officers who were posted to Calcutta probably experienced the quickest disillusion as they sailed for 160 kilometres up a muddy and depressing estuary from which flat and featureless plains stretched out on either side to infinity. If they did not want to put up at an hotel in the city, they were accommodated in Fort William, a huge,

Previous page: A stern-faced Britannia meting out justice

Right: British soldiers by the mosque at the Khyratee gate, Delhi

INDIA IN THEORY.   INDIA IN PRACTICE.

A LAMENT BY ONE OF THE DELUDED.

cavernous building, with long, dark, echoing corridors and barely furnished rooms with stained walls, which lacked any supply of water indoors and had only medieval sanitation. The fort seemed deliberately designed to give the griffin, as the newcomer to India was known for the first year, an unforgettable impression of some of the worst features of Anglo-Indian life. The griffins left as quickly as they could, not only to escape from the discomfort and the general dirt and filth (which was cleaned up mainly by huge storks known as adjutants from their strutting walk), but also because they did not receive any pay until they had joined their regiment.

Although the pay in the Indian army was higher than it was in the Queen's army, so that an impecunious subaltern could just live in extreme and obvious modesty in some up-country station, most subalterns could not live on their pay and were in debt to army agents, banks, or Indian moneylenders who charged extortionate rates of interest. The *Delhi Sketch Book*, an imitation of *Punch* which provided nostalgic humour for ex-patriates in India from 1851 to 1857, published many cartoons on the subject. *The Indian Subaltern's Vampires* shows a young officer with his sword, cap, and belt hanging from a wooden triangle on the

A cartoon from the *Delhi Sketch Book*

78

wall of his barely-furnished bedroom, haunted by the vampire of debt as he lies sleeping in his cot. Another cartoon shows a subaltern heavily burdened with huge parcels of mess bills, bank instalments, and charges for his uniforms, while a third, drawn and written in the 'ye olde Englishe' style of Richard Doyle, who designed and drew the *Punch* cover which lasted for a hundred years, shows 'ye British Subalterns being sick under ye combined influence of bad rations, mess stores and other indigestibles' as he reflected on his 'harde fayte'. In addition to these financial burdens, the need to pass a compulsory examination in native languages seems also to have preyed heavily on the young subalterns' minds.

Initially, before some mental adjustment had been made, the anticipated pleasures and luxuries of Anglo-Indian life seem to have been less than appealing to the griffin. One cartoon in the *Delhi Sketch Book* shows a group of alarmed guests at a dinner party holding their nostrils as an Indian servant takes the lid off a silver tureen with one guest mildly inquiring: 'Doesn't it strike you that the mutton is rather high?' Dysentry, cholera, and malaria all contributed to the delights of Anglo-Indian life and its high mortality rate. The climate was also a source of other illnesses, with many British officers and troops going down with heat exhaustion in the hot season from March to June while the succeeding monsoon season regularly produced its own crop of influenza and fevers. To seek relief from the excessive rain and heat, women and children retreated to the hill stations for five of six months every year, accompanied at one time by their officer-husbands until their leave was restricted by Sir Charles Napier when he was commander-in-chief. Poona was the main hill station for Bombay; Ootacamund, or 'Ooty' as it was affectionately known, for Madras; but the most prestigious station, particularly after it became the summer residence of the governor-general, was Simla in the foot-hills of the Himalayas. With its pleasant climate and its steep hills densely covered with fir and pine trees, it provided a delightful retreat where wives could think lovingly of their brave husbands fighting some savage tribesmen far away or labouring at their regimental duties in the sun-baked plains, while they flirted archly with less committed officers on extended leave or sought better jobs for their husbands from any official whom they happened to have enchanted. There was an endless round of amusements and delights – rides on horseback or in *jampans*, a kind of Sedan chair, along the Mall, picnics on the wooded slopes, polo tournaments and race meetings in the afternoons, and almost every night, dinner parties, balls, and amateur theatricals, a tradition which has endured among British officers stationed overseas in the form of regular performances of Gilbert and Sullivan. But even the elegant delights of Simla, however roseate they may have seemed in retrospect, did not always come up to the expectations of some people who experienced them at the time as we may still see in *Such a Jolly Ball*. This ability to laugh at personal misfortune, which was provoked and sustained by the main Indian imitators of *Punch*, the *Delhi Sketch Book* and *The Indian Punch*, helped to make the lives of many hard-pressed and depressed colonial officers more tolerable.

The status of the Indian army officer was lower than he had expected. In addition to the company's forces, there were always a number of units from the Queen's army stationed in India for a tour of duty, some 22,000 officers and men just before the Mutiny. These Royals, as they were known, were just as contemptuous of the company's officers

Below: A cartoon from the *Delhi Sketch Book*

SIMLA, IN SEASON.

No. II.—*SUCH A JOLLY BALL.*

Above: One of a series of cartoons published by the *Delhi Sketch Book* about 'The Glorious Fun we had at Simla (Season '54)'

as they were of civilians. The *Delhi Sketch Book* published a long series of cartoons, *The Royals in India*. In one of them the 'lady of the house' asks a Royal officer, 'Do you never dance, Captain Baker?' To which he replies with a stunning rudeness which recalls the bad manners of the Tenth Hussars in Dublin: 'Why – ha! – not in India.' Those cavalry officers who did not resign their commissions when they were posted to India – a not infrequent occurrence – retained all their polite, but complacent anti-intellectualism. An elderly civilian asks one of them:

– Pray, Captain Heavysides, what do you think of the present state of the Charter question?
– Why, ve fact is, I've given up finking: I believe it makes ve hair gwow gway and dwop out.

The same sense of contempt for the Indian Army officer infected Royal NCOs and other ranks. It was common for their wives to work as nursery maids for Anglo-Indian civilians, but one corporal's wife, fashionably dressed in a flouncy skirt and a large hat, was forced to reject a job when she discovered her employer's ghastly secret. 'Why, you see m'arm,' she tells a startled Indian officer's wife, 'it isn't the wages which is quite satisfactuary, but I've been and spoke to my husband, and he have objections to my taking service with the lady of a sepoy officer.'

The young subaltern in the Indian army found that in spite of his military bearing and his glorious uniform he trailed far behind civilian employees of the company in the marriage stakes, so that mothers soon put a stop to any shipboard romances which started so frequently on the voyage out to India that the P & O line became known as the 'fishing fleet'. Civilians, known as '£300 dead-or-alive men', because that was their starting pay and their widow's pension, were rated much higher than the humble ensign with his remote prospects. In one cartoon, a 'speculating mama' complains to one of her many marriageable daughters:

> – How stupid you were, Louisa, last night, wasting the whole evening on the Ensign Binks from Barrackpore.
> – Well, I'm sure, Mama, it's not my fault if these military will dress in mufti – how *are* we to know them from civilians?

Fortunately for them, army officers have usually had the gift of laughing at their misfortunes, their brother-officers and, on occasions, even themselves. There is a long tradition of caricature in the army, stretching back to the eighteenth century when England's first notable amateur caricaturist, George Townshend, the fourth viscount, who fought at Culloden and under General Wolfe, made many enemies with his caricatures and his sick humour. When a fellow-officer had his head blown off in battle, Townshend commented: 'I never thought he had so much brains before.' This tradition of mockery – of the peppery colonel with his hookah and his Indian mistress, of the empty-headed major, and the pretentious griffin – endured for many years. One military scrapbook of the 1860s, preserved in the National Army Museum, contains a cartoon of a 'gallant major, commanding a detachment' testily reproving an NCO by inquiring: 'How is this Sergeant. Here is Cholera in the Island and you have not put an extra sentry on the gate.' Many army officers with their trained powers of observation – both military and landscape drawing were taught at Addiscombe – their long periods of leisure between battles and expeditions, and their involvement in a closed circle of definite stereotypes and very distinctive individuals, were encouraged to put down their visions on paper. George Franklin Atkinson, a captain in the Bengal Engineers who produced a superb set of paintings of the Indian Mutiny, also had a considerable gift for caricature as he demonstrated in *Our Griff*. This long British tradition of self-mockery was to reach its peak during the Second World War in such fictional creations as Pilot-Officer Prune and the Two Types, true representatives of the self-derisory British spirit.

Even though 'our griff' was usually forced deeply into debt by his necessary extravagances, he did enjoy a much more luxurious life than he would have had at home. After the initial shocks and disillusionment had disappeared, most of them settled into the routine of the Indian army life with its pig-sticking, polo, and big-game shooting; its gossip, flirtation and occasional scandals, its morning ride before the visit to the club and coffee shop, its tiffin, and its sundowner. Promotion was slow. It took about thirty years to become a major; colonels were very often in their sixties; and many generals were seventy or more years of age, one of them in Bombay being so blind that the main task of his aides was to prevent him from tripping over the furniture. There were always battles to be fought not only in India itself against the Marathas, the Sikhs, the Thugs, and the hill tribes, but also, because of the central strategic position, in many other countries, Malaya, Persia, China, Burma, and Afghanistan, where in 1842 the army suffered one of the worst defeats in its history when a force of 4,500 British and Indian troops were massacred during a negotiated retreat from Kabul, with only one man, Surgeon William Brydon, escaping to tell the tale. Although Indian army officers complained frequently about a vast variety of subjects, including the weather, servants, missionaries, and the political officers of the company who claimed the right to manage military affairs, the magic of India crept stealthily into many of their

A caricature of Our Griff by Captain Atkinson. Even the youngest ensign was expected to have his own bevy of servants and his own 'stud', even if it consisted of nothing more magnificent than one diminutive pony or 'tat' as it was known out East

MOUNTED OFFICERS OF THE BRITISH ARMY IN PEGU.

souls and they came to love the country and its life, if not all of its peoples. Although they might kick a lazy mess waiter and call him, as the *Delhi Sketch Book* archly said, 'a d----d black infidel', many officers had a deep and genuine affection for their sepoys. They listened to their complaints; they learnt their language; they made concessions to their religion and their caste, so that there were often four times as many native camp followers as sepoys when an army went on the march to perform the numerous tasks which were too undignified for the higher-caste sepoys to do themselves. They allowed the Sikhs to continue wearing turbans when they rushed to join the Indian army after their defeat; they allowed infantrymen to wear their own shoes or sandals instead of heavy army boots, even though an order of the commander-in-chief, Bombay, that all sepoys' feet and shoes should be inspected after every march caused a few wry smiles. They abolished flogging for sepoys while it was still used as a punishment for British troops in India. They fought together side by side in battle and often saved each other's lives. They had such faith in the sepoys' loyalty that they would have trusted them implicitly with their own wives and daughters.

But they were to suffer terrible disillusion. The Indian Mutiny was just as unexpected as the Japanese attack on

Typical representatives of the British power in Burma as seen through the eyes of the *Delhi Sketch Book*

84

Pearl Harbor, though both were equally predictable. There
had been mutinies before at Bolarum, Vellore, Barrackpore,
but they were only small compared with the mutiny of
1857–8, which affected the whole of Oudh, central India, and
Rohilkhand. Only the Bengal army was affected; the Madras
and Bombay armies remained loyal, except for a couple of
battalions in the latter. The causes of the mutiny were
manifold: land reforms which struck at the roots of Indian
economic life, the proselytising zeal of missionaries which
threatened Indian religious life, the annexation of states
where there was no heir, or, in the case of Oudh, one of the
two great Moslem states, where there was alleged to be a long
record of misgovernment. Many Indians of different castes,
creeds, and wealth began to feel threatened. Rumour and
fear was rife in princely palaces, native bazaars, and sepoy
cantonments. British rule in the sub-continent had always
depended largely on consent as the vast majority of the army
of a quarter-of-a-million men were native troops. There
were large regions where no white soldier was stationed for
many miles. The sepoy held the key to the continuance of
British power and many of the sepoys in the Bengal army
were becoming disaffected with the withdrawal of al-
lowances for foreign service, as they saw it, in Sind and the
Punjab; over enforced service in foreign wars beyond the
bounds of India; over increasing attempts to preach
Christianity at them and to convert them. Their suspicions
of British rule increased when it became known that the
authorities in London planned to issue them with new
cartridges. In the standard practice of those days, the end of
the cartridge had to be bitten off before it could be used.
Some of the cartridges were greased with cow fat, which is
sacred to Hindus, and others with pig lard which is unclean
to Moslems. The authorities in India soon realised what
offence these new cartridges would give and ordered that
they should be issued only to British troops and that sepoys
should be allowed to grease their cartridges with vegetable
oil or beeswax and to break them with their fingers and not
their teeth.

But the damage had been done. Some sepoys started to
refuse to handle any cartridges, old or new. On 9 May 1857,
at Meerut, eighty-five cavalry troopers who had refused to
load their rifles, were stripped of their uniforms and
marched ceremoniously to gaol in fetters to serve ten-year
sentences for mutiny. On the following day – a Sunday – the
sepoys at Meerut rose in revolt, burning their barracks,
killing British officers, and violating their wives with brands
of fiercely burning thatch. The 60th Rifles were stopped by

mutineers as they marched unarmed to church parade. Ever afterwards, British soldiers in India always carried loaded rifles when they went to church. With Meerut in flames, the mutineers streamed out to Delhi, 65 kilometres away, seized the city, and proclaimed the ancient Mughal Emperor, who had been a pensioner of the company since 1803, as their leader. Revolt soon flared across central India to Cawnpore, where, after the British garrison had surrendered, 200 British women and children were butchered with long knives before their bodies were thrown unceremoniously into wells. At Lucknow, British soldiers and civilians withdrew into the Residency, where they were besieged for many long weeks by rebel forces numbering up to 100,000 men at times. The siege was ended in November 1857, when Sir Colin Campbell, the last commander-in-chief of the company's forces, relieved the town long enough to evacuate the British from the Residency. Its cannon-scarred shell was afterwards preserved as a permanent memorial to British fortitude – and Indian treachery – from which the Union Jack always flew. Meanwhile, in September, Delhi had been retaken after much fierce house-to-house fighting. Large reinforcements of white troops had been brought in from Britain and battles and mopping-up operations continued in many parts of central India before peace was finally restored in July 1858.

When the news of the mutiny first reached London, there was a superior feeling of certainty that Palmerston, who was still in power after bringing victory in the Crimean War, would soon bring the affair to a successful conclusion just as he had done in the past with other natives who had tried to thwart Britain's will. A cartoon in *Punch* shows a smiling Palmerston in the unaccustomed role of 'boots', with a large jug of water in his hand, knocking at the door of a resolute, grim-faced Sir Colin Campbell who is already dressed for military action. 'Here's your hot water, sir,' says Palmerston. To which Sir Colin, a trifle too optimistically, replies, 'All right. I've been ready a long time!' But when the news of Indian atrocities reached England, the mood swiftly changed. Britain, which had only recently been humiliated, if not defeated, in the Crimean War was in no mood to be humiliated again by a bunch of 'damned, black infidels'. *Punch*, which was then in its most magisterial and symbolic phase, shows an angry Britannia meting out *Justice* to rebellious sepoys, but sparing women which was something that the 'half-civilised' Indians had not yet learnt to do.

There was even greater fury in India. For the massacre at Cawnpore and the murder of the young, pregnant Mrs

Sappers at work in the batteries in Delhi, one of George Atkinson's paintings of the mutiny

Chambers who had been hacked to death at Meerut, the British exacted a terrible vengeance. Moslems were hanged with pig flesh stuffed in their mouths; Hindus were forced to lick up the blood of their victims before they were executed; other mutineers were blown from guns – an old Mughal custom – their heads rolling to the ground and their dismembered bodies showering gunners and spectators with flesh and blood. Villages were burnt to the ground; lynching parties terrorised the countryside. This vengeance and retreat from reason did not go entirely unopposed. But the orders and the appeals of the Governor-General, Lord Canning, for clemency found favour neither in Anglo-India nor at home. *Punch* published a cartoon of him patting a diminutive Indian on the head and saying: 'Well, then, they shan't blow him from nasty guns; but he must promise to be a good little sepoy.' Cartoonists have always had a great gift of identifying and inflaming existing popular passions. The bitter hatred for the native population was increased by these hysterical anti-Indian cartoons, which touched the deepest feelings of the xenophobic Victorian middle classes.

In India, the sense of bitterness and betrayal persisted for many years. In 1859, *The Indian Punch* was started, significantly, at Meerut where the mutiny had begun. In one of its first issues, it included what must be one of the most vicious and vindictive cartoons ever published in *Native Infantry Lines*, which simply shows three looped ropes hanging empty from the cross bar of a gallows. Captain Atkinson, whose book of paintings of the mutiny was dedicated by permission to the Queen, wrote in the dedication: 'When a remorselessly treacherous and rebellious foe sought to uproot the British Power in India, and by acts of deliberately planned ferocity and fiendish cruelty strove to destroy every European and Christian in the land, the devoted heroism of a small but resolute force, who fought to maintain the rights of their sovereign and the honour of England, was so far crowned with success as to stay the arm of the destroyer, wrenching from his grasp the stronghold of rebellion, and winning for them not only victory in the crime-stained streets of Delhi, but the proud satisfaction of YOUR MAJESTY'S gracious approval and heart-felt sympathy.' The mingled feelings of relief, anger, pride, and betrayal gushed out in a torrent of words which expressed the general sentiment of Anglo-Indians.

As in other wars against natives, once white supremacy had been re-established, the Victorians allowed themselves the liberty of laughing at their own misfortunes. During the lengthy mopping-up operations, *Punch* showed a typically effete member of the heavy cavalry chasing an armed trooper of the Indian light cavalry. 'I'll give it to you, you miscreant,' the British cavalry officer says, 'when (!) I catch you!' *The Indian Punch* published a retrospective cartoon making fun of the deprivations that some besieged garrisons had had to endure – and of the ignorance of the officers who had come out from England. Feeling more secure again, the Anglo-Indians could at last afford to make some rather heavy-witted puns about the native mutiny. It was 'gross inconsistency' complained *The Indian Punch*, that 'the Brahmins who venerate the Cow, should object to the

The Pàdri of some starved garrison during the Mutinies being accosted by an Officer foraging for his men is told that he could only offer him Chupaties.
OFFICER.—" PATE'S! THE VEWY THING OF ALL OTHERS! BY JOVE, THIS ISN'T SUCH A BARBAROUS COUNTRY AFTER ALL!"

When the mutiny had been crushed, the Anglo-Indians and the army could afford to laugh at their misfortunes again as in this cartoon from *The Indian Punch*

government of John Bull' and 'what an extraordinary race the late Bengal army was composed of, when the sepoys preferred being blown from a gun, to a blowing up from their superior officers'.

But there was great discontent and resentment among the Anglo-Indians at the India Act of 1858 which seemed to give mutinous Indians greater rewards than they obtained for their fortitude and loyalty. The East India Company, condemned in a *Punch* cartoon right at the beginning of the mutiny for its avarice, misgovernment, blundering, nepotism, and supineness, was finally abolished and its power transferred to the Crown and its officers and men to the British army. In an attempt to remove some of the major causes of Indian discontent, the Royal proclamation was weighted heavily in favour of the natives, guaranteeing the princes security, granting some prisoners an amnesty, and giving all peoples freedom to worship in their own way. This encouragement of native religions did not find favour with *The Indian Punch*, not through sectarian reasons but through fears of what the consequences might be in day-to-day life. It published a cartoon showing 'our conscientious sub acting up to the Queen's proclamation' by saying to his 'idle' servant who had demanded yet another day off: 'Aw – thank you – No – One of your feast days, I believe? Mustn't interfere with your – aw – prejudices – and – and that sort of thing – You can go today.' There was even greater bitterness over the priority given to Indian claims for compensation for losses sustained in the mutiny. *The Indian Punch* shows Lord Canning, who became the first viceroy, sitting on the seat of government with his foot resting elegantly on a stool inscribed 'For Native Loyalty' saying to a white factory owner: 'Wait a year or two, man; I'm too busy with the Natives to attend to your claims.' The feelings of many Anglo-Indians at the time were encapsulated in a simple cartoon published in the same magazine, which showed a signpost situated on a bare and desolate beach pointing to England with a caption reading: 'The only road for a wise man of the East to take.'

Some of them did so, including many of the company's soldiers. They claimed with some justice that if they were to be transferred to the British army, they should be paid the normal Queen's bounty when they re-enlisted. But the Treasury refused to pay, maintaining with dubious logic, that as it had decided not to pay the sepoys a bounty, the white soldiers were not entitled to one either. The white troops' resentment flared into mute revolt, and when they were given the option of taking their discharge about 10,000 did so. Many more men had to be recruited in Britain and other soldiers had to be brought back from New Zealand and Canada, not only to replace the soldiers who had taken their discharge, but also to strengthen the white element in the Indian army. By the time the reorganisation had been completed in 1863, there was about one British soldier to every two sepoys to ensure that the loyalty of the army should never again be tested in the same way. At the same time, there was a switch in the recruiting of Indian soldiers from the Bengalis to the Sikhs and the Ghurkas who had remained loyal. It is some tribute to the Indian army and the Indians themselves that such an effective fighting force, which gave such service to Britain in two world wars, should have arisen from the partially burnt ashes of the old.

With no immediately threatening enemies in India itself, the army could concentrate its resources on foreign engagements and on the protection of the immensely long frontier of some 6,450 kilometres which stretched from Assam in the east, to Sind and the Punjab in the west. There was always some sport to be had in these mountainous frontier regions, from small-scale expeditions, which returned in honour and glory after a village or two had been burnt, to larger conflicts such as that on the borders of Assam in 1891, when about 5,000 troops descended on the small state of Manipur to avenge the murder of the chief commissioner of Assam and four British officers. But the main area of conflict was on the north-west frontier with Afghanistan, whose boundaries remained undefined until almost the end of the nineteenth century. In this harsh mountainous region of craggy peaks and broad, burning valleys, about 645 kilometres long and 160 kilometres deep, no law ruled except for the sniper's bullet and the quickness to observe. For once, even the caricaturist's ability to exaggerate could scarcely improve on the extravagance of nature. It was perfect country for the ambitious young officer who wanted action – a permanent field-day with live bullets in hazardous terrain against a fierce and skilful enemy. On average, there was about one fairly large expedition every year and many smaller engagements. It produced many epics of courage and endurance: the heroic stand by Brigadier-General Sir Neville Chamberlain against a much larger force of Bunerwal tribesmen in the Ambela pass in 1863; the relief of the small British garrison in Chitral by Colonel Kelly, who led a 320 kilometre forced march across snow-covered mountain peaks and passes in 1895.

The north-west frontier, however, had a much greater strategic importance than the punishment of recalcitrant

Right: The British jackboot in revenge for the siege of Kandahar

STAMPING IT OUT.

A painful necessity both for John Bull and for the Afghan Scorpion.

tribesmen. By the 1880s, Russia's overland expansion had brought its boundaries right up to the northern frontier of Afghanistan, which thus became the only obstacle between the Russian empire and the British empire in India.

Britain wanted to preserve Afghanistan as a buffer state. To increase its influence, the British government demanded in 1878 that the Amir should accept an envoy at his court. When he refused, the Indian army invaded, and forced Afghanistan to accept their envoy; but four months later the envoy and his mission were murdered in Kabul. Lieutenant-General Roberts, who had commanded one of the three columns in the first invasion, was sent back to avenge the massacre, defeating the Afghans after some fierce fighting just outside the capital of Kabul in December 1879.

He remained there to instal an Amir who was more favourably disposed towards Britain. But in August 1880, Roberts received news of the defeat of a British force in the south of the country and of its withdrawal into the city of Kandahar. Roberts set out with a force of 10,000 men to relieve the besieged city. They marched for almost 500 kilometres across desert and scrub-land in temperatures which rose to over 100 degrees by day and fell almost to freezing point at night in what was one of the quickest forced marches in history. In spite of their exhausting march, the British routed the Afghans and relieved the city. The march became one of the great epics of history which made the Victorians so very proud to be British. There had been some dissenting Liberal voices about the wisdom and the conduct of the Second Afghan War as a whole, but there was nothing but proud gratitude for Roberts's long march to Kandahar. The British public, which was then in its most jingoistic and imperialist phase, loved it. Roberts was made a baronet and received the thanks of the Houses of Parliament and of the Queen herself – and a plethora of tributes for his skill and bravery by the cartoonists in the humorous magazines.

5

THE SUN NEVER SETS

THE BRITISH LION AROUSED.

B. L.:—"DON'T BULLY ME, SIR! I DON'T MIND BEING KICKED BY ONE OF MY OWN SIZE, BUT I'M NOT GOING TO STAND IT FROM A LITTLE NIGGER LIKE YOU!"

The Victorians had plenty of other epic feats of personal courage and fortitude, and many more great victories over 'wogs' and 'fuzzy-wuzzies' to cheer, as there were no less than seventy-two major campaigns and wars – more than one a year – in the Queen's long and noble reign. In the major humorous magazines – *Punch*, *Fun*, *Judy*, *Moonshine* – the British lion appeared as regularly as a circus animal, rampant or crouching, but always fiercely threatening, to give a vicarious thrill each week to the distant spectators. John Bull stamped his high, spurred boots down on any black-skinned creature who was causing him some temporary annoyance, and as a last resort Britannia was ushered out in her flowing robes to flail her sword. Britain was already beginning to feel the first uncomfortable draughts of unfair competition from continental despots, so that these imperial adventures and achievements became of even greater importance and solace, as Disraeli with his statesmanlike cunning realised, allowing the country to bask for a few more decades in the reflected warmth of an empire on which the sun never set. In the second half of Victoria's reign, the middle classes felt a growing need for military supremacy, whether it was achieved by reform or by colonial victories, in what was becoming an increasingly uncertain and hostile world. Their need for assurance was reflected in the smug and sentimental stereotypes of military heroes who dominated the cartoon world during this period.

The Victorian generals, invariably moustachioed, still stare out of the pages of the humorous magazines, stern-faced, bold, and uncompromising, their chests glittering with many decorations. They were idols, the pop stars of their day; indeed, Wolseley was the model for the modern major-general in the *Pirates of Penzance*. Most people had their own favourite general and many of them gained such an intimate place in public affection that they were usually known by their nickname: Wolseley, 'our only general' or 'All Sir Garnet'; Kitchener of Khartoum, 'K of K'; Gordon, 'Chinese Gordon'; Roberts, 'Bobs'. There were many other generals, celebrities in their day, who are now no more than names in military history, such as Sam Browne, who lost his left arm in the Indian Mutiny and who designed a belt to carry his sword and pistol which still bears his name, and General Sir Gerald Graham, who won a VC in the Crimean War and went on to win a great victory over the Sudanese forces at El Teb.

The best generals were expected to be men of great character and personal courage, who not only commanded

Above: Wolseley, 'Our Only General', as seen by *Punch*

Right: A Zulu warrior

Previous page: The British lion's indignant response to the attacks of King Kofi (complete with coffee pot), during the Ashanti war of 1873–4

94

DAYS WITH CELEBRITIES (194).
GENERAL GRAHAM.

their men but actually led them into battle, as General Gordon did, carrying only a thin cane with the same kind of nonchalant bravery which General Gough had exhibited during the first Sikh war when he rode out from the lines in a white coat to divert the enemy's fire from his own troops. Apart from gunners and engineers, most of them were largely untrained and in the main contemptuous of professionalism, so that is is scarcely surprising that there should have been so many near-run things. They sometimes lost their way, stranding their troops in defenceless scrub or desert, as General Hicks did in 1883 in the province of Kordofan in the Sudan, when he and most of the 10,000 Egyptian troops whom he was leading were massacred by dervishes. The charge of the 21st Lancers at Omdurman in 1898, when five officers, sixty-five men, and nearly a third of the horses were slaughtered in two minutes, ranks with the Charge of the Light Brigade at Balaklava for military ineptitude and reckless folly. Earlier, in the Zulu War of 1879, Lord Chelmsford, the commander-in-chief, had left the base camp of his central column unfortified at Isandhlwana, while he went out on reconnaissance with the result that it was overwhelmed by a strong force of 14,000 Zulu warriors, who massacred most of the British and native soldiers. Although the distant spectators often had to live for weeks or months in doubt, grief, or anticipation of further disasters, victory in the end always went to Britain with its overwhelming strength and resources. The conclusion of each campaign was celebrated with an end-of-term jollity and a sense of a better tomorrow, so that Lord Chelmsford was pictured in *Judy* sitting stoically on a rock, while Britannia, trampling on the unfair accusations of 'ignorant criticism' gives him a friendly pat on the shoulder, like a kind housemaster consoling a boy who had scored a duck in his last match at school. The caption reads: 'Well done, Chelmsford.'

The Victorians, however, were far less smug and self-satisfied than we have been led to believe. Beneath their pose of effortless superiority, they were very often anxious, inquiring, worried little men full of doubts about themselves and their society. After the disaster in the Crimea, there was always a great sense of disquiet about the army, so that in the following fifty years it was the subject of no less than 550 official investigations. One of the chief problems was the constant shortage of recruits. Some of the old sources flowed less freely since so many Irishmen had died or had emigrated during the potato famine, while the young men in the Highlands had become more resistant to the patriotic

General Graham VC, one of the great Victorian military heroes, who has now been virtually forgotten by the general public

THE ARMY OF THE FUTURE.

DEDICATED TO THOSE WHO WOULD IMPROVE ITS POSITION, BUT ARE AFRAID TO PAY THE PROPER PRICE.

The Victorian army found it
increasingly difficult to
attract recruits in peacetime

appeals and proffered bounties of the lairds than they had
once been. The army, with its low pay, its floggings, its
twenty-one-year commitment, was even less attractive to the
very kind of English recruit that it most needed, as skilled
craftsmen were just beginning to gain a better standard of
living. The patriotic appeal of such music-hall songs as *The
Soldiers of the Queen* had little effect in making men accept
the Queen's bounty. The working class man, like those idle,
insolent maidservants, was beginning to lose some of his
former deference and to become more aware and cynical. In
one cartoon published in *Fun*, a recruiting sergeant asks a
likely-looking man:

> – Want to 'list, my man? You're just the smart sort o' chap we
> wants!
> – Oh, indeed – lost yer colonel then, have ye? Well, I'll think
> about it and let ye know.

Starved of sufficient funds to pay its recruits a good wage, the
army was unable to fulfil all the roles that its civilian
taskmasters, but reluctant paymasters, demanded. It never
had enough men to protect British bases in all parts of the
world, to perform police action in colonies, to fight colonial
wars, and to provide defence at home, so that occasionally
Britain had to be left virtually undefended. There were
insufficient troops, even with the aid of the Indian army, to
fight colonial wars on two fronts, as was clearly demonstrated in 1885 when troops had to be withdrawn from the
Sudan to counter a new threat elsewhere. Britain was even
less prepared to take on a major European power. Prussia,
which conscripted its young men for a three-year period, had
been able to field an army of 400,000 men against Austria in
1866. At that time, Britain with its traditional opposition to
conscription, had an army of 135,000 and only a few
thousand in reserve. In 1867 two new reserves were created –
a first reserve of 20,000 regulars and 30,000 militia recruited
for a five-year term, and a second reserve of 30,000 men
composed mainly of pensioners. The scheme was not a great
success.

With the growth of Prussia's military might and its three
successive victories against Denmark, Austria, and France,
there was a lurking fear that Britain might soon be forced to
engage in a continental war again. In *Fun*, John Bull,
accompanied by a bulldog in a spiked collar, says to
Cardwell, the Secretary of War, 'It is possible I may have to
go to the continent shortly, so you must pack my carpet-bag
immediately, and be sure you put in everything that may be
necessary.' But Cardwell's bag of reforms looked more
useful than they actually proved to be. He tried to increase

the number of recruits by shortening the length of service from twenty-one to twelve years, of which six years were spent with the colours and six with the reserve; he gave soldiers a pay rise of a shilling a day; and he abolished flogging except in times of war. An attempt was made to forge new links between the regulars and the militia by bringing them together in new regimental county depots, which he hoped would also encourage recruitment. But the most controversial change was his abolition of the purchase of commissions.

The House of Lords was incensed by Cardwell's proposal. Control of the army by purchasing commissions had enabled the aristocracy and the landed gentry to retain the ultimate power in the country. About half of all commissions in the army were held by members of these groups and virtually all the rest by members of the upper middle classes. The House of Lords threw out Cardwell's Bill at first, though they eventually passed it after he had threatened to introduce it by royal warrant. Even so, he had to pay black market prices in compensation to the army officers, and not the official rate, for buying out commissions. There was some premature jubilation in the ranks when purchase ended on 1 November 1871. In a *Fun* cartoon, an Irish private, with the gift of the blarney, tells his nursemaid-sweetheart:

> Shure thin, darlin', isn't this the blessed furrust o' November, and ivery man in the ridgmint is as good as another, from the officers downwards? So if ye'll only consint, it's meself that'ull make ye a cyaranal's lady in no time at all, at all!

In fact, the change made scarcely any immediate difference to the composition of the officer class. Men who held commissions were not only officers, but also gentlemen, who were expected to hunt for two days every week in some regiments, to play polo, to gamble, and to dance, so that young officers in the cavalry needed a private income of at least £600 or £700 a year, and even in regiments of the line they needed a minimum of £100 a year. Regiments became in some ways even more of a club with entry restricted to those young men who had been to the right public schools, which had taken on the task of running both the civilian and the military sides of the empire. In some of the more prestigious regiments, the proportion of aristocratic officers actually increased after the abolition of purchase. Eight years later, in *Judy*, a captain in the regulation mufti outfit of bowler hat and subfusc suit with narrow lapels, who has gone down to Brighton for some diversion, tells two young ladies how he invariably spends his days: 'Oh, King's Woad in the

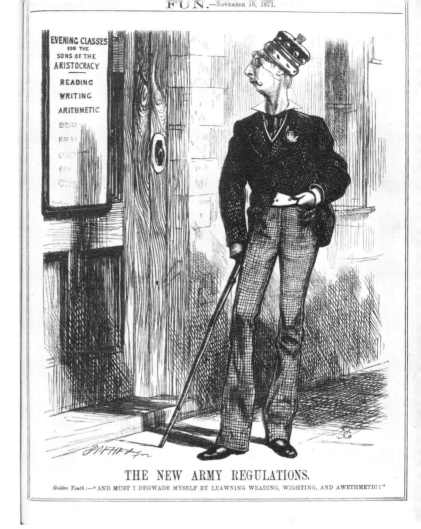

THE NEW ARMY REGULATIONS.

Golden Youth :— "AND MUST I DEGWADE MYSELF BY LEAWNING WEADING, WIGHTING, AND AWETHMETIC!"

The educative results of abolishing the purchase of army commissions

morning or wide – aquarium after lunch – theatre or billiards after dinner.' There had not been much change.

Cardwell's reforms also failed to produce many more men despite the aid of the army's best recruiting sergeant, unemployment, who stalked the whole countryside as Britain plunged into the worst agricultural depression of the century. The army with its unreasonable 'bull' and unthinking discipline still failed to appeal to the majority of young men. There was a well-worn joke about army discipline which had first appeared in *Fun* in 1864 and which was still being repeated in *Comic Cuts* in 1896:

> OFFICER: Why haven't you shaved, you dirty fellow?
> SOLDIER: If yer please, sir, I'm growing my whiskers.
> OFFICER: Oh, you are, are you? Well, you've plenty of time to do that off parade. Two days' pack-drill!

The lack of recruits and an increase in desertions, illness, and foreign commitments continued to thin the ranks at many regimental depots. A *Punch* cartoon of 1873, *Out o' Soldiers*, shows an adjutant reporting 'All present, sir' to his commanding officer, with just one soldier on parade in the vast barracks square. Many men also opted out of the militia for various reasons. *Punch* showed a captain of 'a rural corps' calling over the rolls. 'George Hodge,' he shouted. 'George Hodge! Where on earth's George Hodge?' To which a voice from the ranks replies: 'Please, sir, he's turned dissenter and says fighting's wicked.'

In the initial flush of enthusiasm for reform, the first large-scale manoeuvres were held in Britain in 1871; but they provided more copy for *Punch* than serious military training. It is Wimbledon, at midnight. A mounted volunteer officer rides up to a sentry outside a tent.

> – Hullo, here. Why don't you turn out the guard? I'm the field officer of the day.
> – Then what the deuce are you doin' out this time o' night?

The average Briton just did not provide suitable material for army 'bull' and mock wars, and the manoeuvres were abandoned after only a few years. Further attempts at reform were obstructed for many more years by the reactionary Duke of Cambridge, who had become commander-in-chief at the end of the Crimean War and who clung obstinately to office until he was manoeuvred out in 1895 at the age of seventy-five. Cardwell had tried to get rid of him or to limit his powers, but it was not easy to undermine the authority of a first cousin of the Queen. Despite the reforming efforts of politicians and the mockery of cartoonists, the army had not undergone any really radical surgery, and it emerged from its ordeals in much the same state of health as before, ready and fit to undertake colonial wars, but still incompetent to take on white adversaries, as was to be demonstrated later in the disastrous Boer Wars.

These final golden years of imperial glory, when Britain was still respected and even feared in all corners of the globe, produced the last old-style battles and epic feats of endurance and courage which still arouse nostalgic pride. Clad in his red coat, though in some campaigns this was replaced by khaki, the British soldier hacked his way through dense jungles, marched through parched deserts, scaled mountain peaks to fight the Queen's enemies wherever they were to be found – in Abyssinia, Persia, Perak, South Africa, Egypt, the Sudan, West Africa, the North-West frontier. He stood brave and undaunted in the same kind of formal battle square which had proved so effective against the charges of the French cavalry at Waterloo, and fired his volleys with the same kind of disciplined regularity as his forbears had done at Blenheim. Even though he had been armed since 1871 with the .45 Martini-Henry rifle, which was replaced in 1888 by the .303 Lee-Metford, and the first modern machine-gun, the Maxim, in the following year, while the enemy sometimes had nothing more formidable than matchlocks and spears, the British soldier was fighting in unfamiliar terrain and often had to face an overwhelming superiority of numbers.

Despite occasional setbacks, the Victorians excelled in these colonial wars. In 1873–4, Wolseley gained the first of his great victories in Africa against the Ashanti tribes living in the interior of what is now the state of Ghana. The Ashantis had become a threat to other tribes living nearer to the British forts on the coast. Wolseley was forced to construct over 200 bridges on his long march through densely-forested, hilly, and unhealthy country to the Ashanti capital of Kimasi. After a model victory over the Ashanti tribes, Wolseley forced their paramount chief, King Kofi to pay an indemnity before he returned to England, and a hero's welcome.

Five years later, Wolseley was sent back to Africa to fight the Zulus. The war had started badly with the massacre of British troops at the unfortified base camp of Isandhlwana. This disaster, however, was redeemed on the very same day by the heroic defence of the mission station at Rorke's Drift, a ford on the river Tulega, by a company of just over a hundred men under the command of a young lieutenant. Using flour bags and biscuit tins as parapets, they repulsed wave after wave of Zulu warriors from the late afternoon until dawn, saving, in the words of *Punch* 'not only a colony, but the credit of old England' and bringing eternal glory on themselves which was recognised by the award of seven Victoria Crosses. Some 10,000 reinforcements were sent out from England under the command of Wolseley; but before they arrived, Chelmsford had redeemed his earlier failures and blunders by massacring a force of 20,000 Zulus at Ulundi in half-an-hour. The Zulu warrior king, Cetewayo, was captured, but not knowing quite what to do with him, Britain restored him to power only three years later.

In 1882, Wolseley returned to Africa yet again, this time to the north, with a much larger force of 40,000 men. Anti-European riots in the bankrupt state of Egypt, fomented by Colonel Arabi, the Minister of War, threatened British financial interests and Britain's new lifeline to the East, the Suez Canal. Taking the Egyptians by surprise, Wolseley landed at Ismailia on the Suez Canal, and after a night march through the desert, routed Arabi's forces at Tel-el-Kebir, north-east of Cairo. *Punch* celebrated this further victory of the 'modern major-general' in appropriate imperial style with a cartoon entitled *Vici!*, which shows Wolseley standing stern and erect over Arabi grovelling on the ground, while in the background victorious British troops cheer and wave their pith helmets on their bayonets in the air. To safeguard British interests in the country, Egypt was made a protectorate.

The British takeover in Egypt led to further imperialist wars. There was soon a revolt against Egyptian rule in the Sudan led by the self-styled Mahdi or Messiah. Gordon was sent out to the Sudan to evacuate civilians and Egyptian troops, but after he had despatched the first group of 2,000 he decided to remain in Khartoum and to hold it against the rebel dervishes. The siege began in March 1884, with Gordon defending a triangular wedge of the city, protected on one side by the White Nile, on the second by the Blue Nile, and on the third side by a 5 kilometre-long ditch and ramparts, which he further fortified with land mines and barbed wire entanglements.

At home, Gladstone, who had never been enthusiastic for imperial adventures, even though he was increasingly forced into them against his will, was reluctant to send out a relief force, considering that Gordon had betrayed his trust by converting his mission from peace to war. But there was such a great public outcry for aid to be sent to their beleaguered hero that Gladstone eventually relented. Britain's 'only general', Wolseley, was once again despatched to Egypt, arriving in Cairo early in September. Owing to adminis-trative muddles, the start of Wolseley's march to Khartoum was delayed. He had to fight two savage battles on the way, at Abu Kru and Abu Klea, where a British square was broken for the first time in these colonial wars. Meanwhile, Gordon, his supplies of food almost exhausted, watched anxiously through his telescope on the roof of his palace-headquarters for the first signs of the relieving force, but all he saw was the preparations of the Mahdi for the final assault. Gordon was killed on 26 January 1885, when a huge force of 40,000 dervishes broke through the defences which had been partially levelled when the Nile had flooded. Two days later, the first steamer of the British force sailed into Khartoum. Back home, public sorrow at the unnecessary death of their great mystical hero was only matched by indignation and disgust at Gladstone's long delay in sending relief. In *Moonshine*, Gladstone was portrayed crawling up to Wolseley in the desert and saying: 'Too late for Gordon and the rest. Never mind – save me – save Downing Street.'

Gordon 'sacrificed' at Khartoum. To us, this cartoon in *Moonshine* may look like an advertisement for indigestion tablets, but to the Victorians it symbolised all their feelings of imperial honour and glory

Gordon's death was finally avenged on 2 September 1898, when the dervishes were routed at the battle of Omdurman, across the river from Khartoum, with a loss of 11,000 dead against only 500 British casualties. The army was led by Kitchener, another great Victorian military hero, who had been appointed Sirdar, or commander-in-chief of the Egyptian army at the early age of thirty-nine. He had taken his time to reconquer the Sudan, gradually moving his force of 15,000 men up the Nile in stages over a two-year period. After the victory at Omdurman, a funeral service for Gordon was held at the ruins of his palace and the British and Egyptian flags were flown from the roof.

Kitchener then marched on south to occupy the rest of the Sudan, when to his surprise he encountered a small French force occupying Fashoda on the Upper Nile, which they had reached after an eighteen-month march across the continent from the French Congo. For a time there was great tension between Britain and France; but after some intense diplomatic activity, the French agreed to withdraw and to renounce all claims to the Nile valley. Britain then set up a joint government with Egypt, which was merely a nominal partner, to rule over the Sudan. It had been another great victory, this time against a major European power, without a single shot having been fired.

These great Victorian military triumphs were celebrated in the traditional way in the weekly humorous magazines and in the increasing number of other publications which were by then using cartoons. The total repeal by 1861 of all the Taxes on Knowledge – the advertisement, stamp, and paper duties – had produced a flood of new papers and periodicals, including some humorous magazines such as *Fun* – the poor man's *Punch* – which was started in that year and *Judy*, which began publication six years later. From 1868, *Vanity Fair* had been publishing caricatures – coloured lithographs of prominent people of the day by 'Ape' (Carlo Pellegrini) and 'Spy' (Sir Leslie Ward). Cartoons also appeared occasionally in other publications including the *Graphic*, the *Sketch*, and *Truth*, which employed F. Carruthers Gould to illustrate the Christmas issue of 1879. By 1890, the first cartoonists were working regularly for newspapers in both London and the provinces, and three years later, the *Daily Graphic*, the first fully illustrated daily paper in England, sent the cartoonist, Phil May, on a world tour. This newspaper was also the first to make extensive use of the new photographic method of reproducing line drawings on a zinc plate, which made it much quicker to print cartoons and gave

Sir Francis Carruthers Gould (1844–1925) was the first daily cartoonist on a London newspaper. Born in Barnstaple, the son of an architect, he started work in a local bank at the age of sixteen. Five years later he went to London to work in a stockbroker's office and after a few years he became a broker himself. He had already gained something of a reputation as an amateur cartoonist among his friends and his colleagues in the financial world, and in 1879 he was asked to illustrate the Christmas issue of *Truth*. He continued to do so for a number of years until in 1890 he was appointed caricaturist on the *Pall Mall Gazette*. Three years later, after the paper had changed its owner and its politics he moved to the Liberal *Westminster Gazette*, where he worked until the First World War. He was made assistant editor in 1896 and was knighted for his political services when the Liberals came to power in 1906. He was pre-eminently a political cartoonist, and although his draughtsmanship was undistinguished, he had a facile gift for catching the likeness of a face and a great inventiveness of ideas.

the artist greater freedom as he was no longer dependent on the services of the wood-engraver. Half-tones, which allowed photographs and shaded drawings to be reproduced, were being used by the *Daily Graphic* only four years later, and they soon became common in many magazines, with *Punch* publishing its first half-tone illustration in 1896.

Most of the cartoons in these publications were traditional in style and in attitudes, deriving in the main from *Punch*; but there were also new magazines which had a completely different kind of cartoon. The Education Act of 1870 had produced a whole new generation of working-class literates and semi-literates who were as keen as the middle classes to have humorous magazines of their own which reflected their values and attitudes and their own anti-authoritarian brand of humour. The first distinctive working class cartoons appeared in illustrated comics which were originally published, not for children, but for adult members of the working classes – artisans, shop assistants, and clerks. *Funny Folks* had been launched in 1874 and was followed ten years later by *Ally Sloper's Half Holiday* which went on being published until 1923.

Ally Sloper, who had first appeared as a cartoon character in the pages of *Judy* in 1867, was the original comic anti-hero, a bald ne'er-do-well with popping eyes, a crumpled face, and a bulbous nose, who was always sloping off down the alleys of the East End with the police in hot pursuit after he had been involved in some shady business deal such as

Right: Cartoonists in the early comic papers allowed their imagination to take off into realms of fantasy. Here two war correspondents, Airy Alf and Bouncing Billy, are lending Kitchener a hand at Fashoda

The Big Budget. 1d

VOL. III. No. 70. WEEK ENDING SATURDAY, OCT. 15, 1898. PRICE 1D.

AIRY ALF AND BOUNCING BILLY TAKE FASHODA.

1. WHEN the Sirdar sent back all the war correspondents, Alf and Billy objected. "Look here, Willyum," lisped Alf, "the BIG BUDGET'S goin' ter 'ave some noos from the front." "Ree-light-o!" said Billy. "I'm game. Gee hoop, me Arab steed."

2. But when those camels streaked straight for Fashoda with the patent seasick sixpence-a-sail trot, the bounders objected again. "Drop it, yer double-'umped, frog-faced switchback," roared Alf. And Billy gurgled piteously : "Oh, me pore bones."

3. Of course those "ships of the trackless desert" couldn't stand such language. They promptly wrecked themselves, and the crew got washed overboard. Bump! Billy struck the sand. Thump! Alf did likewise. "Enough ter give a billiard-table the hump, ain't it?" gurgled Billy.

4. The camels had strolled back to Khartoum for tea, so the dauntless ones had to foot it to Fashoda. They reached it and rang the bell. "Vat vos you vant?" hollered a voice. "We've come ter stay a bit, old French polish," lisped Alf and Billy. "Open the door."

5. But those Fashoda gents weren't having any, and Alfie and Willyum got mad. Alf made a speech, while Billy, who's a champion at the game, picked the lock. Then they hopped in and made things hum. "Biff 'em," shrieked Billy. "Kokernut or cigar, sir, good shot!"

6. In about two ticks and an eighth Fashoda was taken. Next day the Sirdar turned up. "Wot cheer, 'Erbert," sniggered the town-takers, "we've got a little present for yer—caught 'em orl ourselves. If yer don't make us dooks yer're no class." Strangely enough the Sirdar didn't seem to like it.

Published at the Offices of the BIG BUDGET, 28, Maiden Lane, London, W.C.

starting a shark loan club – his very first exploit – or opening an illegal betting shop. His success encouraged other entrepreneurs to produce comics for the new mass market. *Jack and Jill* appeared prematurely in 1885 as the first illustrated comic for children, but after a few issues had to expand its market to include adults, too. In 1890 the young Alfred Harmsworth launched *Comic Cuts*.

The comics provided a continuous story in cartoon form. They were packed with action in the form of 'biffs', 'bangs', and 'booms'; they had regular characters like Weary Willy and Tired Tim in *Illustrated Chips* and Airy Alf and Bouncing Billy in *The Big Budget*; and from about 1900, they had speech balloons instead of captions, reviving a tradition which went back to the days of the great Georgian caricaturists. These strip cartoons were very different from the sedate, middle-class political and social cartoons. They introduced a new note of working class fantasy and irreverence in which reality and dramas were inextricably mingled. These ageless cartoon characters with children's minds travelled far and wide to lend a hand in their own inimitable way to any hard-pressed general. Airy Alf and Bouncing Billy assisted Kitchener at Fashoda; Weary Willy and Tired Tim with their 'noble army of unwashed wanderers' aided 'Sir Reddy' by 'spifflicating' the Boers; and Bounderby Bounce helped Kitchener and Roberts in South Africa. Their fantastic adventures were often terminated by a fall into unwelcome reality, but they survived to have another go in the next issue. Not unnaturally, there was a marked change in the attitude to the common soldier in the illustrated comics; he was no longer someone to be pitied or ignored, but a man to be admired, to be laughed with. The age of Everyman – and conscription – was dawning.

6

VICTORY AT A PRICE

THE SCHOOL OF MUSKETRY.

The Victorian army staggered to extinction on the scrubby, eroded veld of South Africa, though fortunately for Britain a new, modern, and more efficient army was swiftly created almost as soon as the disastrous Boer War had ended. The war revealed that however successful the army might be in fighting 'wogs' and 'fuzzie-wuzzies', it was no real match for intelligent and resourceful white opponents. It took more than two-and-a-half years for 450,000 troops, including some contingents from the Dominions, to defeat 50,000 Boers. All the shortcomings of the army in structure, training, strategy, and equipment were mercilessly revealed not only to the British and the Boers, but also for the whole world to see. By the end of the war Britain's military and diplomatic prestige had reached its lowest point for many decades. The post-war inquest – the report of His Majesty's Commissioners on the War in South Africa – is one of the most damning indictments of the army ever published.

There would have been more excuse if the army had not already come up against the Boers eighteen years earlier, in 1881. Even though the first Boer War had been ended by Gladstone for political reasons only three months after it had began, the army had suffered two resounding defeats at Laing's Nek and at the nearby Majuba Hill, which Sir George Colley hoped to seize so that he could outflank the Boer positions. Colley's force was routed and he was killed. Shortly afterwards Gladstone made peace and granted the Boers in the Transvaal self-government. During the brief war, the cartoonists had been quick to observe the superior skills of the Boers in marksmanship and in mobility; but neither the government nor the army had noted or managed to benefit from the lesson.

On 11 October 1899, President Kruger declared war on Britain, and his forces armed with German rifles and artillery, invaded the British colonies of Bechuanaland, Natal, and the Cape. The second Boer war had begun. Although it had been obvious for many months that war was virtually inevitable, the government had refused to reinforce the small garrison of 15,000 men in South Africa, fearing that it might upset the protracted negotiations with the Boers. A fortnight before war was declared, the government finally sent out 43,000 reinforcements under the command of Sir Redvers Buller, one of Britain's top generals, who had served in China, Egypt, and the Sudan and who had won a Victoria Cross in the Zulu war. Three days after the war had begun, he sailed from Southampton in the *Dunottar Castle* and was given the usual circus farewell in the funny

Previous page: The Boers give the Duke of Cambridge, British commander-in-chief, a lesson in sharp-shooting in this Tenniel cartoon published in *Punch* in 1881

Left: An observation balloon about to take off during the siege of Ladysmith

Acts Now, Not Words.

Mr. CHAMBERLAIN (to Sir Redvers Buller, leaving for the front: "Good-bye, Redvers; hope you'll be back soon. Am sure your arguments will have more effect upon Kruger than mine."

Left: A cartoon by
J. M. Staniforth published
in the *Western Mail*,
Cardiff, at the outbreak
of the Boer War

Below: Another work by
the same artist,
prematurely celebrating
the British victory at
Glencoe Hill

magazines by the British lion, the British bulldog, and Britannia, the inventive powers of most cartoonists having been very nearly exhausted by these annual salutes to departing generals.

In Britain there was the usual euphoric mood of determined patriotism and confident optimism which flushed the face and heart of the British public at the start of every Victorian war. In *Punch*, a heavyweight John Bull, with his sleeves rolled up, warns a cruiserweight Kruger in plain English: 'As you *will* fight, you shall have it. *This* time it's a fight to a finish.' Young officers were convinced that it would be an easy war. One subaltern in *Fun* which might more aptly have been named *Pun*, is being seen off by his Aunt Tabitha at a railway station:

> – Goodbye, my boy! Do try to instil into the poor Boers a few civilised ideas.
> – Oh, yes, aunt: we shall soon introduce to them some of our best English 'Maxims'.

Disillusioned.

THE BOER (going down Glencoe Hill): "Ach, mine kontempt for Tommy Atkins vos not so great now as it vos!"

Victory at a Price

Another 'very young subaltern' in *Punch* tells a fellow-officer why he is taking all his polo sticks to South Africa: 'Well, I thought we should get our fighting done by luncheon-time, and then we should get the afternoon to ourselves and could get a game of polo!' The British workman expressed his optimism in a different style. After studying a large-scale military map of South Africa in a publishers window, he tells his mate: 'See that pink, Bill? That's our'n. See that green? That's their'n. *It'll all be pink soon.*'

There was great self-congratulation and jubilation back home when the first reports from the front seemed to indicate that the nation's easy optimism was about to be justified, with the capture of Boer positions and guns at Glencoe, north-east of Ladysmith; but later reports showed that it had not been such a great victory as it seemed to be,

A Raven-Hill cartoon published in *Punch* at the start of the war

First Bystander. "AH! THEY BE NOBLE BOYS, THEM SODJERS, GOIN' AN DYIN' FOR THEIR COUNTRY."
Second Bystander. "SHURE, AN' ISN'T THAT THE WAY THEY MAKE THEIR LIVIN'?"

Leonard Raven-Hill
(1876–1942) is a somewhat under-rated and neglected cartoonist. He was born in Bath, the son of a stationer. Despite initial opposition from his family, he was determined to become an artist and studied in London and in Paris, where he exhibited paintings at the Salon in 1886. He then turned to drawing, and worked for numerous magazines, including *Punch*. He became a staff member of that magazine in 1901 and political cartoonist after Sambourne died in 1910. In 1935, he retired because of ill health. A rapid, facile draughtsman, he had a greater gift for social than political caricature. His later work was marred by his failing eyesight, which probably accounts for his diminished reputation.

since General Symonds had been fatally wounded in the battle and a whole squadron of the 18th Hussars had been captured by their imprudent eagerness to finish off the fleeing Boers who had set a neat little ambush for them. By 1 November the Boers were already besieging British forces in Mafeking on the borders of Bechuanaland, Kimberley on the borders of Cape Colony, and Ladysmith in Natal. It soon became obvious that it was not going to be a fair, sporting war. The Boers used white flags to lure gullible British soldiers within range of their sharp-shooters' rifles; they refused to stand still so that they could be shot, but had the unsporting habit, as Kitchener himself later complained, of unfairly slinking away on their little ponies without giving the British soldier any chance to open fire; and they hadn't even had the decency to wait for British reinforcements to arrive before they started investing towns.

Sir Redvers Buller, who had gone out from Britain with such a high reputation, soon had it shattered into the dry South African dust by the Boer marksmen. On his arrival, he split his forces into three columns. Between 10 December and 15 December – 'Black Week' as it came to be known – all three columns, including his own, suffered resounding defeats with total losses of nearly 3,000 men. At home, this unwelcome Christmas present produced general gloom. Were Cecil Rhodes in Kimberley, Baden-Powell in Mafeking, and Sir George White in Ladysmith to suffer the same fate as Gordon at Khartoum?

But the British are always at their best when they are staring real disaster in the face. Before 'Black Week', there had been no more enthusiasm to volunteer for service overseas than there had been in any previous colonial war.

Many civilians still felt that the army was a remote body which had very little to do with them, a feeling which was encapsulated in a cartoon by L. Raven-Hill published in *Punch* on 25 October 1899. The three consecutive military disasters in 'Black Week' produced a great change in public attitudes. In all parts of the country, patriotic volunteers rushed to join the colours, lured out perhaps by their repressed yearnings for glory and adventure.

Their sudden descent upon the recruiting offices revealed that it was not only the army which had been allowed to decay in Victorian times, but also the flesh and blood which could have provided it with much-needed recruits. Years of exploitation, bad food, bad housing, and lack of medical care had produced a generation of undersized and unhealthy young men, suffering from a wide variety of physical defects – squints, deafness, crippled limbs. In Manchester, for instance, 8,000 out of 11,000 volunteers had to be rejected outright and of the remainder only 1,200 were passed as A1. As these crippled and diseased volunteers limped into public view from their slums, the establishment was just as horrified and shocked as it had been by the military defeats. It vowed that never again should there be another generation of such sorry, physically-unfit recruits, and decided to provide all children, not with better food or medical care, but with barrack-square drill and military discipline. Immediately the war had ended, peripatetic NCOs were seconded to teach military drill, based on the new military training manual which had just been issued by the War Office, to Board school children in their playgrounds and to some of their middle-aged schoolmistresses in draughty depots and open fields. Another wartime proposal that schoolchildren should be trained to use rifles was taken somewhat less seriously.

Even though the army stood in such dire need of recruits, it could not help strangling itself from time to time with its own red tape. There was great indignation in the pages of *Fun* when it was revealed in June 1900 that a Guards' reservist, who had volunteered to fight the Boers, was to be prosecuted for the technical offence of failing to fill in a form to draw his reservist's pay. The Westminster magistrate was not amused either. He was compelled by law to fine the man £2, but he ordered that it should be paid out of the poor box.

Within a few days of 'Black Week', Buller had been dismissed from his post of commander-in-chief, but he was not recalled, and went on to lose two more bloody battles with heavy British casualties, the first at Spion Kop on 24 January 1900 and the second at Vaal Krantz only twelve days

Cadet Corps.

CADET TOMMY : "How have you got on for marks, Billy ?"
CADET BILLY : "Oh, stunning ! Two for arithmetic, three for spelling, twelve for drilling, fifteen for strategy, and twenty for shooting !"

A cartoon from the *Western Mail* satirising a proposal to train all schoolboys in the use of arms

later. He had been replaced as commander-in-chief by one of the greatest, first-division players, the veteran hero of many great Victorian engagements, Field-Marshal Roberts of Kandahar, who for good measure had Lord Kitchener of Khartoum as his chief-of-staff. Roberts arrived in Cape Town on 10 January 1900. With a quick appreciation of the situation, he decided that mobility was the key to success. Despite opposition from more conservative generals, he formed units of mounted infantry which could move around the vast battlefield as quickly as the Boers, while some of the Australian contingent who had come over to help Britain in its hour of need, later adopted an even more novel form of speedy transport by riding special tandem bicycles which ran on the railway tracks.

Roberts's strategy, energy, and determination produced quick results. Kimberley was relieved on 15 February 1900, and Ladysmith on 28 February by Buller who had at last partially redeemed his honour. There was immense relief and joy when the news of these long-awaited victories reached England, where Sir George White, the defender of Ladysmith, had become something of a hero. Since

1 November he had suffered daily bombardments from the large Boer force; he had fought off numerous attacks; he had made two major sorties against the investing force; and he had ignored Buller's earlier order made in 'Black Week' to surrender. White was much admired for his laconic messages which he sent out in quick succession, with their characteristically modest understatement which had such a great appeal for true-born Englishmen: 'Hard pressed' – 'very hard pressed' – 'enemy repulsed at all points'. When Ladysmith was eventually relieved, *Punch* charitably forgave Buller for all his previous blunders. It published a cartoon showing Sir George White and Sir Redvers Buller clasping hands in front of a tattered, but still intact, Union Jack. The caption read:

> – I hoped to meet you before, Sir Redvers.
> – Couldn't help it, general. Had so many engagements.

There was even greater excitement in Britain when the last of the invested towns, Mafeking, was relieved on 17 May 1900. For more than seven months a small force of 1,000 men had held out under the inventive command of Colonel Baden-Powell, who made his own artillery out of drainpipes and organised the life of his garrison so thoroughly that he even issued his own banknotes. When the news of the relief of Mafeking reached Britain, London and many provincial cities exploded in a spontaneous celebration of joy, which added a new word, mafficking, to the language. Excited crowds of Londoners singing 'Soldiers of the Queen' and 'Rule Britannia' swarmed into the West End from the City where the news had been first announced by the Lord Mayor of London, who had assured his audience in a short speech that 'British pluck and valour when used in a right cause must triumph'. Strangers shook hands with each other in the streets; flags appeared from nowhere; and cab drivers shouted out the good news. In Liverpool, church bells rang, and bands played in the streets. There were similar scenes of unrehearsed joy in many other cities including Newcastle, Birmingham, Plymouth, Bradford, and Leicester. A cartoon in *Punch* shows a flag-draped reveller singing to himself when he arrives home at 3 am:

> VOICE *(from above)*: Good gracious, William. Why don't you come to bed?
> WILLIAM *(huskily)*: My dear Maria, you know it's been the rule of my life to go to bed shober – and I can't poss'bly come to bed yet!

Punch could not conceal its pleasure that the Boer was on the run at last and published a rather infantile war conundrum in celebration. Within a short while, the news

All the excitement of the attempt to relieve Ladysmith spilled over into the comics, which frequently published special military issues in their early years

VOL. VI. No. 141.   WEEK ENDING SATURDAY, FEBRUARY 24, 1900.   PRICE ONE PENNY.

Sir Redvers Buller, V.C., Commander-in-Chief of the Ladysmith Relief Force.

Sir Geo. White, V.C., Chief Commander of gallant Ladysmith, to whom this number is dedicated.

Sir Charles Warren, Commander of a Ladysmith Relief Force.

The brave garrison of Ladysmith watch the approach of their Comrader-in-Arms. Cheers ring out, and the guns are manned. Is relief at hand? It is a terribly anxious moment; but, stand or fall, Ladysmith has won the admiration of the world. May they have the good luck they deserve!

from the front was even better. Roberts's victorious army, which had already captured Bloemfontein, the capital of the Orange Free State, swept on to take Johannesburg on 31 May and Pretoria, the capital of the Transvaal, on 5 June 1900. The two Boer states were then annexed to Britain. Even though Roberts was by then an old man of sixty-eight, he had more that justified his reputation as a field commander and he returned in triumph to Britain in November 1900, to succeed Wolseley as commander-in-chief.

It had been an arduous campaign against a resourceful and determined enemy in unfamiliar and difficult terrain inhabited by an unbowed and hostile civilian population. Although the excellent Boer marksmen claimed many British victims, the vast majority of men died from disease, particularly typhoid fever, caused by polluted water supplies and poor sanitary arrangements, which infected more than one in ten of all the troops involved. This was even less excusable than it had been in the Crimean War, as the War Office had already been offered an effective inoculation against typhoid by the great pathologist, Sir Almroth Wright, but had promptly rejected it.

The ravages of disease, the extremes of climate, the hostility of civilians, and Boer marksmanship and ambushes were what most British officers and men remembered from the Boer war. One officer, Samuel M. Rowlandson, a land agent who served with the Durham Light Infantry, kept a cartoon sketchbook of his experiences in South Africa which can still be seen in the National Army Museum. His main concerns were the flies and the mosquitoes; the

A rather feeble war conundrum by Bernard Partridge in *Punch.* The caption read: 'What operas does the above sketch call to mind – 'Cavalleria Rusticana', 'Der Fliegende Holländer'

Sir Bernard Partridge (1861–1945) came from a family with artistic connections, an uncle being a famous portrait painter and his father professor of anatomy at the Royal Academy. He started work as a stained glass designer and then became an actor, working for Henry Irving and Forbes-Robertson, before he decided to devote himself to cartoons. Joining the staff of *Punch* in 1891, he became chief cartoonist in 1909 and was knighted in 1925. He continued to work for the magazine until his death in 1945. A better draughtsman then Tenniel, his work is distinguished for its theatrical effect, which may have been encouraged by his early experiences as an actor. He was the last great representative of the conventional, anecdotal *Punch* cartoonists, a tradition which stretches back through Tenniel to Leech.

extremes of climate with torrential rain, whirlwinds, and excessive heat which set the veld on fire; the hostility of the civilian population; but most of all the mysterious ability of the Boers to materialise in the most unexpected places, from behind a rock in the middle of the veld or on a hill above kaffir kraals, which had become Boer tourist traps for newly-arrived officers.

It was a very different kind of war, particularly in its later stages, from any that Britain, or indeed any other country, had ever fought before. The new smokeless powder, which had been intoduced in the previous decade, allowed the single, silent marksman to remain undetected in his hiding place. For the same reason, distant artillery became much more difficult to spot, even though balloons were used for observation as they had been during the Napoleonic wars. The nature of war itself was also beginning to change. It was no longer merely a conflict between opposing armies; the British had to fight a whole, united nation in which soldier and civilian merged almost imperceptibly into one. Even though the Boers had fallen into the old-fashioned trap of besieging towns, they helped to make war more mobile than it had ever been before. The old pitched battle, with opposing forces ranged against each other in classic, parade-ground style was becoming increasingly anachronistic and so was the nameless automaton, drilled to fire one volley after another from his static lines. At the very time when new technological developments, particularly the Maxim machine-gun, were beginning to transform war into a holocaust, the soldier was becoming far more of an ordinary human being trapped in extraordinary circumstances but with thoughts and feelings of his own.

This humanisation of soldiers was reflected in the cartoons. Although the soldier was still sometimes portrayed in allegorical terms as he was also to be in later conflicts, his flat image was being filled out with more human sentiments. The comments on war were becoming increasingly oblique. In *Punch*, a trooper who has just caught a locust shows it to his mate. 'Look'ere, Bill,' he says. 'This is a rummy country. 'Ere's the bloomin' butterflies in khaki!' With the greater emphasis on individuality, the NCO, who had in practically all previous cartoons merged indistinguishably with the men, begins to acquire characteristics of his own. With the greater authority which was accorded to him, he replaces the officer as the men's main enemy, confounding, terrorising, and baffling soldiers and recruits with his repartee and often incomprehensible orders. In *Judy*, a line of recruits in civilian clothes, some with rifles and some without, is being

A cartoon by the other Rowlandson, an amateur cartoonist in the army, entitled 'A stealthy infantry patrol'

drilled by an NCO. 'On the command quick march,' he bawls, 'the recruits will swing the left arm freely, and those without arms will swing both!' Reality and reportage were beginning to replace invention. The cartoonists had become more specific and technical in their self-imposed task of keeping the army on its toes. Although they were still willing to cheer any British victory and to execrate the foe, there was much less sentimentality in their views and fewer stereotypes, reflecting the changes which had occurred in real life, as Britain and other countries moved into a more technical and complex age.

The Boer War did not end with Roberts's great victories. In fact, the longest and most arduous part was yet to come. In November 1900, Roberts, who was a great field commander but had little appreciation of the deeper motives underlying war, returned home, after handing over to his chief-of-staff, Kitchener, in the confidence that the war had been won. But for another eighteen months, Boer commandos under their brilliant, fast-riding commanders like de Wet, Botha, and Smuts, continued to inflict casualties on detached British columns and to interrupt transport and supplies. Kitchener evolved a ruthless policy of containment which has been much copied in subsequent guerrilla wars. He sealed off large areas of the countryside with blockhouses connected by barbed wire entanglements and trenches so that the commandos could be flushed out from their hiding places. He burnt Boer farms and seized cattle so that civilians could no longer offer succour to the guerrillas and he herded woman and children into concentration camps where some 20,000 died from disease. His task was not simplified by the poor quality of so many of the cheap remounts which the War Office provided for his cavalry and mounted infantry, but in the end his ruthlessness and the sheer weight of British numbers forced the Boers to make peace in May 1902. As had happened after the Indian mutiny, one of the first acts of the government was to provide the former enemies with millions of pounds to compensate them for their losses. The Boer republics of the Transvaal and the Orange Free State were made British colonies, but only five years later they were granted self-government again.

Ironically, the ultimate military consequences of the war were beneficial. The army's performance led to one of the most wide-ranging inquiries and series of reforms for centuries. In 1902, the army finally shed its famous red coat except for ceremonial occasions and with it many of its cherished beliefs and ancient attitudes. Its soldiers were trained in new tactics and fieldcraft and were equipped with improved rifles and guns. A Committee of Imperial Defence was set up; the War Office was thoroughly reorganised; and a general staff system was instituted. To enable the army to face a continental foe again, Haldane created an expeditionary force of six infantry and one cavalry divisions after he became War Secretary in December 1905. He also set up the Territorial Army and formed a special reserve out of the old militia, so that by 1914 the army was better prepared, equipped, trained, and organised than it had been for centuries. The only issue which had not been faced was conscription which had to be resolved in the course of the First World War.

7

LAUGHTER FROM
THE TRENCHES

"'ARF A 'MO' KAISER!"

Previous page:
Bert Thomas's famous
First World War cartoon

The First World War was so horrific in its enormous casualties; its verminous, stinking conditions and its barbarous weapons, including poisonous gas and flame-throwers, that it still astounds imagination. After the intitial battle of Mons, the first battle that the army had fought in western Europe since Waterloo, the British and the French were compelled to retreat towards Paris, which was saved by the battle of the Marne. Five weeks later, in the first battle of Ypres, the British stopped the Channel ports from falling into German hands. By the end of 1914, the war had reached stalemate, with an unbroken line of trenches, stretching for some 650 kilometres from the Channel to the Swiss mountains, manned by the huge conscripted armies of Germany and France and by the much smaller British professional force of just over 100,000 men, though it was to be greatly swollen in size by volunteers – well over 1,000,000 by Christmas 1914 – and by conscripts

"YOUR COUNTRY NEEDS YOU"

Above left:
British trenches
on the Aisne

Above: The most famous recruiting poster of the First World War which has been transformed into a caricature in the minds of later generations through a change in standards and values

from 1916, when Britain acknowledged that it could create a modern mass army in no other way.

The war in the trenches was the most unimaginative, wasteful, and unproductive, except of death and permanent injury, which has ever been fought. Conscription, and the gradual improvement in general living conditions in the years preceding the war, had provided the mass armies; the beginnings of modern technology in the form of aeroplanes and Zeppelins, tanks, improved machine-guns, flame-throwers and chlorine, phosgene, and mustard gases provided the means for exterminating them. On both sides, many officers and men were so greatly appalled by the wasteful slaughter of the best part of a generation that their minds were permanently scarred by the memory. Some of the trenches were so close that in any silent minutes of the night the opposing troops could overhear each other's conversation. In the first few weeks, on one section of the front, enemy soldiers sportingly rigged up targets for each other and shouted out the results, and during the first Christmas many more sang carols to each other. But, on average, the trenches were separated by some 350 metres of 'no man's land', which gradually became a barren wilderness

Below: The disparaging humour of this *Punch* cartoon is typical of the changing British attitudes to war

Tommy (*to his pal in middle of charge*). "LOOK OUT, BILL. YOUR BOOTLACE IS UNDONE!"

of mud, pock-marked with huge shell craters, shattered trees and blood-stained, barbed wire entanglements strung with bloated corpses. For nearly four years, the Germans and the Allies fired bullets, mortar, and high-explosive shells at each other, some of them with a chalked message 'May it have a happy ending' on the base. There were some enormous onslaughts, preceded by a week of heavy bombardment so that the enemy had adequate time to prepare for the attack: the second battle of Ypres in the spring of 1915, when the Germans used poison gas for the first time; the battle of the Somme, from July to November 1916, when the British introduced their slow-moving secret weapon, the tank, which travelled at less than a mile an hour; and the third battle of Ypres from July to November 1917, sometimes known as the battle of Passchendaele, from the name of the town 8 kilometres away which marked the limit of the Allied advance. The slaughter in these battles was immense. Earl Haig, who became British commander-in-chief on the western front at the end of 1915, has been much criticised ever since for these enormous losses, and, indeed, Lloyd George, who became prime minister in 1916, was so appalled that early in 1918 he deliberately retained over half-a-million

Below: A *Punch* cartoon of 1916 which is still as funny now as it was then

Waitress (to Tommy home from the Somme). " HAS YOUR FRIEND BEEN WOUNDED ? "
Tommy. " OH NO, MISS. HE CUT 'ISSELF SHAVING THIS MORNING."

soldiers in England to prevent Haig from resuming the offensive. Nearly three-quarters of a million Britons were killed during the war, the majority on the western front.

The soldier in the trenches needed something to laugh at as desperately as he wanted leave in Blighty. To cater for his need many new humorous publications were started. *The Passing Show*, which appeared on 20 March 1915, was a cheaper kind of *Punch*, costing only a penny, whose regular cartoonists included Edward Tennyson Reed, one of *Punch's* own stars, George Whitelaw, and Leo Cheney. *Blighty*, subtitled 'A Budget of Humour from Home', appeared on 31 May 1916, for free distribution to members of the forces with the help of subsidies from private firms such as Keith Prowse. It contained a number of cartoons reprinted from magazines and newspapers back home and also original contributions from Servicemen. 'Be as funny as you can,' advised the art editor, 'but do not ridicule Fritz too bitterly; you might be captured with a copy of the paper in your pocket.'

By this time a number of national and provincial newpapers already had their own regular cartoonists. Will Dyson had been employed by the *Daily Herald* since 1911 and Sidney Strube by the *Daily Express* since 1912. The public demand for cartoons was becoming insatiable. Indeed, during the war, there was such an immense curiosity to know what other nations were feeling and laughing at that many newspapers started to publish foreign cartoons, unconsciously encouraging the development of a great international business of the future. *Reynold's Newspaper* published a popular feature every Sunday, 'Points of View in Cartoons', which reproduced the best examples from the world's press, including some from neutral countries such as the Netherlands and the United States, before it entered the war in 1917, and, surprisingly, even some cartoons from the enemy countries of Germany and Austria. Censorship does not seem to have been so stringent on either side as it was in the Second World War. One of the cartoons republished by *Reynold's Newspaper* from a German socialist magazine, showed a large gun converted into a corn reaper, and a caption reading 'The Wish of the Nations for 1916'. It also republished cartoons from the leading German satirical weekly, *Simplicissimus*, founded in Munich in 1896, which became the main outlet for anti-British propaganda during the war.

Although the old-style allegorical cartoon with its circus animals and labelled parts continued to be produced in abundance by such artists as Frank Holland who worked regularly for *John Bull*, there were far more cartoons in a new naturalistic style showing soldiers as real live men and not merely as symbols. The soldiers were still caricatured as generalised types, but they were recognisable human beings with thoughts, fears, and hopes of their own, a great development from the bowed, mindless drudges who appear in the background of Gillray's *Fatigues of the Campaign in Flanders.* With the increasing democratisation of the modern age, they had claimed the foreground. One of the most successful cartoons of this new kind, *'Arf a Mo', Kaiser*, which raised a quarter of a million pounds for charity, was the work of a *Punch* artist, Bert Thomas, who, like some other cartoonists, was serving with the Artists' Rifles, which had been founded by Lord Leighton in 1859. But the most famous and the best-loved cartoon soldier of the war was 'Old Bill', a short man with a walrus moustache, a pudgy nose, and a philosophic cast of mind, who was created by Captain Bruce Bairnsfather.

The son of an army officer, Bairnsfather was commissioned as a second lieutenant in 1911, but soon resigned his commission to study art at John Hassall's school in Kensington, and then gave that up, too, to become an electrical engineer. When the war broke out, he rejoined his

Charles Bruce Bairnsfather (1888–1959) became a cartoonist as a result of his experiences in the trenches during the First World War. Born in Murree, India, the son of an Army officer, he attended the United Services College, Westward Ho!, which had provided Kipling with his material for *Stalky and Co.* He joined the Royal Warwickshire Regiment as a second lieutenant in 1911, but soon resigned his commission to study art. Deciding that he was no better fitted for an artist's life, he became apprenticed to a firm of electrical engineers.

On the outbreak of the First World War, he rejoined his regiment and was posted to the western front, where he started sketching and drawing cartoons. His creation 'Old Bill' brought him world-wide fame. In December 1916, he was attached to the Intelligence Corps as an officer-cartoonist.

Although he continued drawing cartoons for English and American publications after the war, he never repeated his phenomenal success. During the Second World War, he contributed a feature, *Then and Now*, to *Reveille*, with updated versions of his First World War cartoons. In 1942, he was appointed official cartoonist to the United States Army in Europe.

"There goes our blinkin' parapet again."

old regiment, the Royal Warwickshires, and was posted to France in November 1914. He began sketching in the trenches at Messines and his first cartoon *Where did that one go?* was immediately accepted for publication in the *Bystander*. He was wounded in the second battle of Ypres, and after a period of recuperation in England, returned to the western front. Later, he was made an officer-cartoonist in the Intelligence Corps. Old Bill, as Bairnsfather writes in his autobiography, *Wide Canvas*, was neither a 'deliberate creation' nor based on an individual soldier, but 'slowly created himself'. His two mates, Bert and Alf, also materialised in much the same way. Although Old Bill was immensely popular with soldiers and civilians from the moment of his conception, there was a small minority who thought that he was prejudicial to discipline: one humourless MP even asked in the House of Commons whether this 'vulgar caricature of our heroes in the trenches' should not be banned.

It is easy to understand why these cartoon characters were popular in the trenches since they helped to distance soldiers from reality by transcribing their extraordinary experiences into the terms of normal life again. The soldier is not running away from the German bombardment, but from a wasp; the hole is not a shell hole, but a cage for a canary; the rats are to be feared more than German bullets; the former shop manager – a real civilian in uniform – shouts out 'Shop' when he has to turn out the guard; the old soldier approaches the German parapet not to attack but because he may have left his pipe there in the retreat. One *Punch* cartoon showed a soldier, drenched with rain, sitting on the edge of the trench and complaining that the beastly Belgian tobacco and the blooming French matches will be the death of him. Two soldiers, up to their knees in water, console themselves with the thought that they don't have to put up with all the winter slush and mud in London streets – or the increased price of whisky. The humour had become a shield against reality. Even Old Bill himself and other cartoon Tommies were part of the deception, because they were very much older than most of the soldiers who still stare youthfully out of newspaper advertisements or who sing merrily in photographs as they march cheerfully towards the front for the first time. The increase in age helped to limit pity.

A musty smell arose from some cartoons as there is an age-old continuity in military humour and soldiers' concerns. The 'flannel coats of mail' cropped up again in many cartoons with baffled soldiers holding up some misshapen knitted comfort from home for public inspection and

133

derision. Food had always been of obsessive concern to soldiers and there were many jokes about the unending issue of plum and apple jam and about GHQ sending urgent messages in the middle of an offensive to discover how many tins of jam had been issued in the previous week. Old Bill was usually so hungry that he could be easily diverted from his observation duties to peering through his binoculars at German soldiers munching sausages.

Sentry duty was another ancient topic. In *The Passing Show*, an orderly officer on his rounds at night asks a nervous sentry why he has failed to challenge. 'P-please, sir,' he replies, 'I d-didn't know who you was, sir.' The duty produced a new kind of nervous apprehension on the western front, when the silence might be disturbed only by the distant chattering of machine-guns and some scarcely-heard or imagined scuffling, which might just be rats again or might be a German patrol which at that very moment was about to leap over the parapet. Bairnsfather became a master of suspense at night, with all its small sounds and hazy visions, displayed in the agitated fears of *The Fatalist*, and of the nervous sentry, who is only reassured when he hears the friendly reply to his challenge: 'You shut yer ---- mouth, or I'll ---- come and knock yer ---- head off!'

As Kitchener's appeals to patriotism enticed hundreds of thousands of recruits into the war machine, the NCOs, with their waxed moustaches and their pot bellies, loomed larger and larger in life and in the cartoons, their mouths opening wider and wider, their language becoming coarser and coarser as they tried to instil some of the military virtues into the straggling line of slovenly and inept recruits. 'Keep your heads up there,' they shouted. 'You're not looking for fag ends now.' And that was the mildest form of abuse. In the early months of the war, many of the NCOs were true figures of fun themselves, decrepit veterans, with hazy recollections of their battles against the Zulus, the Egyptians, and the Boers, who had been dragged out of retirement to train recruits armed with broomsticks in a new kind of trench warfare which they had never experienced. This poor training, which may have helped to increase casualties on the western front, was just one of the many consequences of the nation's long-standing refusal to accept conscription in peace time. The NCOs' contempt for these raw recruits was surpassed only by their scorn for officers. 'Why,' bawls one exasperated sergeant in *Blighty*, 'I've seen hofficers what 'ad more brains than some of yer.'

The new mass army with its growing, if still unspoken spirit of civilian defiance and egalitarianism, brought about a

Right: Bairnsfather was a master of the comic tensions of night-time life in the trenches

The Fatalist.

"I'm sure they'll 'ear this damn thing squeakin'."

radical change in the attitudes to officers which found release in the wish-fulfilments of cartoons. There were no great cartoon generals as there had been in Victorian wars. Kitchener, who had been appointed Secretary for War on 7 August 1914, and was drowned on 5 June 1916, when his ship hit a mine while he was on the way to Russia, received some of the traditional tributes in the humorous magazines. Haig put in one or two appearances, particularly in the old-style cartoons; but the death of Roberts, who caught a chill a few days after he had gone out to France at the age of eighty-two to command the large Indian contingent, passed virtually unnoticed. There was no interest either in the one general who might have been expected to have attracted some interest in the new mass army – Sir William Robertson who had risen from the rank of private to general and who was Chief of the Imperial General Staff from 1915 to 1918. In the cartoons, the generals tended to merge into anonymity, distinguishable only through their facility for falling into holes and trenches, and by their enormous moustaches. Officers were no longer the brave individual heroes that they had once been, but caricatured stereotypes with physical characteristics denoting rank: the clean-shaven second lieutenant; the bemonocled captain; the colonel with his large waxed moustache. Their punctilious insistence on being saluted even in the most inappropriate circumstances, a demand which was most pronounced among civilians turned junior officer for the duration, was the butt of much cartoon humour.

It was not only generals who were mocked and ridiculed, but also the machine, which had mown down all the old concepts of military honour and glory. William Heath Robinson's secret weapons – armoured bayonet-curlers, corn crushers, and shell diverters – delighted both civilians and servicemen who sent him many suggestions for further inventions and continued to do so long after the war was over. Some of his inventions, such as the use of laughing gas to soften up British troops before an attack, foreshadowed the use of more deadly varieties by the Germans; while some British inventions, such as a machine for throwing grenades into German trenches, was so reminiscent of his impractical, but ingenious, inventions that it became known as the Heath Robinson gun. Some of the real weapons of war, however, were still too strange and awesome to arouse much humour. There were relatively few jokes about flying, even though the Royal Flying Corps, which had only about 150 aircraft mainly for reconnaissance in 1914, had expanded so rapidly that by 1918 it had no less than 22,000 which were used in a

Right: A Heath Robinson cartoon – the armoured bayonet-curler for spoiling the temper of the enemy's steel

William Heath Robinson (1872–1944) was determined from an early age to be an artist like his father who was the principal illustrator on the *Penny Illustrated Paper* for many years. He went to the Islington School of Art and the Royal Academy schools. After trying his hand at landscape painting, he began to do book illustrations, including those for an edition of the *Arabian Nights* in 1899 and for the *Poems* of Edgar Allan Poe in the following year. He had already gained a high reputation for his humorous drawings in the *Sketch*, the *Bystander*, and other magazines before the First World War; but it was his caricatures of the machinery and weapons of death during the war which finally established his world-wide reputation. He was the first caricaturist to choose inanimate objects, instead of people, as the victim of his satire.

After the war he continued to contribute humorous drawings to many English and American periodicals, and to illustrate books. He also designed scenery for the Alhambra and Empire theatres in London.

variety of roles including tactical support of troops and bombing.

The civilian population suffered more than in any previous war. They were bombed for the first time, initially by Zeppelins, or 'baby-killing machines' as the *Daily Sketch* called them, and later by aircraft, but these were only small-scale raids in which about 1,000 civilians were killed. Their losses in other spheres were more severe. Income tax was increased from 5.8 per cent to previously unknown heights, 15 per cent by 1916 and 25 per cent in the following year. Luxury taxes were introduced on many items ranging from clocks to cars. There was great inflation, which halved the value of the pound in the four years of war, and so much profiteering that a special excess profits tax was introduced in 1915. As the war went on, many consumer durables, such as furniture, clothes, and shoes, started to become scarce as they were to later in the Second World War.

But the chief topic of cartoon concern on the home front was the growing shortage of food, caused by the ruthless German submarine attacks on both British and neutral ships, which eventually brought the Americans into the war in April 1917. Germany had started its U-boat campaign against shipping in the western approaches to Great Britain early in 1915; but it desisted for a time when the sinking of the liner *Lusitania*, with the loss of over a hundred American lives, brought a stern warning from the President of the

United States, Woodrow Wilson. In 1917, the Germans resumed their unrestricted attacks over a much wider area, with extremely heavy losses among both allied and neutral shipping. There were increasing shortages of some foods in big cities, caused sometimes just as much by poor distribution as by actual scarcity; queues began to form early in the morning at food shops; and there were increasing complaints in the queues and in cartoons about hoarding by 'food hogs'. Food shortages became so severe that, in the cartoons, the remaining domestic servants, who had not escaped from the daily drudgery of their lives into the munition factories, were forced to inform the favourite Bobby on their beat that they could no longer invite him in to eat a plate of cold meat filched from their mistress's table. In middle-class restaurants, little, well-dressed girls complained that they had been given a dirty plate, only to be corrected by their mothers, who informed them that it was the soup; while at home little boys sitting at bare tables protested that they never got that nice, sick feeling any more. To ensure that everyone got fair shares, rationing of sugar started on 1

Below: The amazing man in his flying machine, vintage 1916. A cartoon by E.G.O. Beuttler from his book, *Humour in the Royal Navy*

AN AEROPLANE RISING FROM THE FLYING DECK OF A SEAPLANE CARRIER

January 1918, and it was soon extended to butter, margarine, jam, tea, bacon, and meat.

Women played a much bigger part in the war effort than they had ever done before. They put on khaki uniforms to serve as clerks, typists, and telephonists with Queen Mary's Army Auxiliary Corps in Britain and abroad. The two other branches of the Services also had their own women's auxiliary corps. Thousands of women served with FANY, the First Aid Nursing Yeomanry and with the VAD, the Voluntary Aid Detachment. They worked on farms as members of the Women's Land Army and took over many jobs which had previously been done solely or mainly by men, on the platforms of trams and buses, in print shops, in offices, and behind the wheels of lorries and motor-cars. Later on, as the labour shortage worsened, women took over many heavy jobs, driving heavy overhead cranes and working concrete mixers and stone crushers, though they were employed only as 'substitutes' so that men could claim these jobs back after the war. Many thousands of women emerged from damp basement kitchens, where they had been employed as domestic servants, to gain better wages, greater independence, and self-respect as workers in munition factories. Their great contribution to the war effort was celebrated in many old-style allegorical cartoons in middle-class magazines, which only a few years before had depicted these same women as idle, impertinent, and improvident wretches, in their white aprons and servant's caps, doing their best to avoid any heavy work.

Passions ran much higher on the home front than in the trenches with shirkers, strikers, and the Kaiser as the main targets of abuse. Little old ladies, with thin determined lips, furled umbrellas, and tight-fitting hats, roamed the streets of every city handing out white feathers indiscriminately to any young man who seemed to be of a suitable age for military service, though their short-sightedness sometimes made them choose inanimate victims. Strikes were outlawed in 1915 and the official union leaders accepted compulsory arbitration in disputes; but many unofficial strikes were organised by shop stewards, particularly on the Clyde, where a militant Workers' Committee was set up by shop stewards in the shipbuilding industry. Similar committees were formed in other industrial centres. On average, over 4,000,000 working days were lost each year through unofficial strikes between 1915 and 1918. Lloyd George adopted a conciliatory attitude towards the strikers, but the middle classes were outraged. In 1916, *Punch* reverted to a theme which had been used by its Indian counterpart after

'German "Freedom of the Seas"' – a cartoon from *The Passing Show* of 20 May 1916

Near-sighted Old Lady (a keen Recruiter). "Now look at that young fellow. A couple of months in the Army would make a new man of him!"

the Mutiny by publishing a full-page cartoon showing a bare hillside with an empty noose swaying in the wind with a brief, explicit title 'For Traitors'. There were many cartoons in other publications with a similar theme: a soldier returning from the trenches to tell a munition worker that the army were not allowed to strike; a striker, the 'Kaiser's friend', being viewed benevolently by the German Emperor.

But the most intense hatred was reserved for the Kaiser himself, and for the Germans who were alleged to have slaughtered babies, massacred innocent hostages, and boiled bodies to make soap. In the early months of the war, *Punch* published several special supplements, consisting of collections of past cartoons, to show how Armageddon had been ordained by history: 'The New Rake's Progress', illustrating the Kaiser's career from 1888 to 1914, on 16 September 1914; 'Punch and the Prussian Bully' on 14 October; and 'The Unspeakable Turk' just before Christmas, on 16 December. This hostility to the Kaiser and his minions, however, was so far surpassed by the even more uncontrolled hatred in some ephemeral publications that it makes the *Punch* supplements seem insipid. The Kaiser was depicted as 'The Wild Beast of Europe' surrounded by all his atrocious works, including the sinking of the *Lusitania* and of hospital ships, the destruction of cathedrals, the massacre of millions in Armenia and Belgium, the murder of prisoners, the poisoning of wells, and the spraying of the

Above: Short-sighted old ladies sometimes made a mistake in their selection of likely-looking recruits as in this *Punch* cartoon

Right: A Will Dyson cartoon of the Kaiser, with a caption reading: 'Any orders today, Sire?'

142

Will(iam Henry) **Dyson** (1880–1938) was one of the most distinguished immigrants from the southern hemisphere who have contributed so much to the British newspaper cartoon. Born in Ballarat, Australia, he worked for the Sydney *Bulletin* before he came to London in 1909. He worked as a freelance for many London newspapers and magazines, but he was most closely associated with the *Daily Herald,* whose socialist principles he shared. During the First World War, he became an official war artist on the western front. On his return to London, he worked for the *Daily Herald* again until he returned to Australia in 1925.

Although he continued to draw cartoons, he started to do more serious work, too, and exhibitions of his etchings were held in New York and in London. During the depression, Dyson renounced pure art for politics, and returned to London in 1931 to help the *Daily Herald* in its socialist cause. He continued to work for the paper until his death. All of his work is informed by his deep hatred of snobbery, greed, and militarism.

wounded with gas and liquid fire. In other ephemerae he was shown as the anti-Christ of Armageddon and a Jackal of 'The Beast'.

It was left to more eminent cartoonists to produce equally hostile but more controlled representations of the Kaiser and to bring out all the misery, waste, and horror of modern war. In the finely-drawn cartoons of Edmund J. Sullivan, with their swirling lines and mass of detail, the skeleton of death is always stalking, playing martial drums, or dancing triumph-antly. Will Dyson, the Australian socialist cartoonist, also produced some powerful attacks on the Kaiser. But the most notable anti-German cartoonist was Louis Raemaekers who left his neutral homeland of Holland to live in England and to work for the allied cause. His incessant attacks infuriated the Kaiser so much that he reputedly offered him a large bribe to stop publishing them. Raemaeker's cartoons were univers-ally popular on both sides of the Atlantic, but beneath their hatred of the Germans there was an even more fundamental hatred, as there was in all these cartoons – of war itself.

8

TOTAL
WAR

THE ANGELS OF PEACE DESCEND ON BELGIUM

After the most expensive war in its history with a human cost of over 2,000,000 casualties and a financial cost of nearly £6 billion, Britain almost immediately reverted to its traditional policy of getting defence on the cheap again with as little involvement as possible. It trusted in the Royal Navy to protect its supply lines and its shores from enemy attacks and in the newest star of the Services, the Royal Air Force, to win any future war unaided by massive, strategic bombing. In 1919 the government adopted a 'ten year rule', proposed by Winston Churchill who was then Secretary for War and Air, under which defence was planned, and expenditure curbed, on the assumption that there would be no major war for ten years, a policy which was repeatedly renewed until events in other countries forced a change in 1932. Stringent Treasury control of defence spending, general retrenchment particularly after the Great Depression, Labour opposition to military expenditure, and widespread pacifist public opinion all combined to reduce the strength of the Forces. The 'war to end all war' had temporarily produced a global revulsion against armed forces and nowhere more than in Britain with its long-standing, anti-militarist tradition.

Even when Britain started to rearm in 1935, after Hitler had reintroduced conscription in defiance of the Treaty of Versailles, the army was still greatly neglected. Exaggerated estimates of German defence spending and air strength, and a blind British faith in the invincibility of the bomber, ensured that priority was given to the RAF. By 1939 it was being given more money than either of the other two branches of the armed forces, though fortunately some of it was used to develop a radar network to warn of approaching enemy planes and also to build Spitfires to shoot them down. The Royal Navy in 1939 was still on a par with the United States Navy, the biggest in the world; but many of its ships were out of date and of increasingly limited value, and no new battleships had been built in the years between the wars. The army, starved of money and of public respect, was in a worse shape than it had been at the outbreak of the First World War, so that it took thirty-three days to send four divisions to France in 1939 against fourteen days in 1914, while the armoured division, which had also been promised, did not arrive at all, mainly because the only fully-equipped division was in Egypt and the other two in England were still awaiting delivery of tanks.

Through no fault of its own, the army had become isolated from the nation yet again so that like any closed community it veered even more sharply towards self-involvement, remi-

Previous page: A David Low cartoon published in the *Evening Standard* on 10 June 1940

Right: Hitler taking the salute at the Nuremberg rally in September 1938. Rudolf Hess can be seen on the left of the photograph

"WE ARE PRESENT AT THE END OF COLONEL BLIMP" — *SAYS CRIPPS*

Sir David Low (1891–1963), one of the most forceful cartoonists of modern times, was born in Dunedin, New Zealand. His first cartoon was published in the Christchurch *Spectator* when he was only eleven years of age. In 1911, he went to Australia and became the staff cartoonist on the Sydney *Bulletin*. After the First World War, he came to London and worked for the *Star*, and then for the *Evening Standard*, where he continued to be employed for twenty-three years.

He was a man of immense courage and personal conviction, who was not afraid to attack the Nazis and other totalitarian dictators; the English establishment personified in Colonel Blimp; union conservatism represented by the TUC carthorse; or even his own employer, Lord Beaverbrook, who appeared in some of Low's cartoons as a grinning gnome. More than any other cartoonist, he did most to restore the vigour and the general appeal that caricatures had had in Georgian times.

In 1950, he left the *Evening Standard* for the *Daily Herald*. Three years later, in semi-retirement, he joined the Guardian, contributing three political cartoons a week. He was knighted in 1962.

The funeral of Colonel
Blimp in 1942, as seen
by his creator, David Low

niscence, and conservatism. Colonel Blimp, who was created by David Low, became renowned in the interwar years, as the epitome of military reaction. With his inverted-v moustache, his characterless face, and his swollen paunch, which he was always trying to reduce by skipping, squash, and archery, he pontificated pompously from his Turkish bath on the evils of education, unions, and socialism and any other disturbing change which had occurred during the last hundred years. He had his own quick solutions to all the problems of the modern world. If education was abolished, people would not be able to read about the depression, so that confidence would be restored. Unemployment could be cured by taking a leaf out of Hitler's book and making the workless build concentration camps for their own incarceration. Colonel Blimp was given a mock funeral after the fall of Singapore in February 1942, a defeat which the cartoonists, and much of the general public, attributed to the conservative military establishment of the inter-war years.

David Low, who was knighted in 1962, was the outstanding political cartoonist of the interwar and wartime years. A child prodigy, who was already contributing cartoons to local newspapers in his native New Zealand while he was still an eleven-year-old schoolboy, he left for Australia at the age of twenty and became one of the most controversial and respected cartoonists there. In 1919, at the age of twenty-eight, he went to England and joined the London evening newspaper, the *Star*, leaving in 1927, at the invitation of Lord Beaverbrook, to work for the rival *Evening Standard*, where he continued to be employed until 1950.

Mass-audience cartoonists had come a long way since the days of *Illustrated Chips* and *The Big Budget*. Paid and licensed by the great newspaper proprietors, they had become such a sales asset to newspapers and such a great force in their own right, that Beaverbrook continued to employ Low even though he sometimes disagreed with his views. In the interwar years, the political cartoonists still had great power to mould public opinion. The kind of person who might now be persuaded to change his views by a television interview or a documentary, could be converted by a cartoon then. Low, like many other cartoonists, such as George Grosz and John Heartfield, had seen the writing on the wall while politicians were still trying to persuade Hitler to act like a gentleman. He started to attack Hitler immediately he came to power as Chancellor in 1933 and became so greatly hated by the Nazis that they had his name on the death list of people who were to be executed when they had occupied Britain.

During the war the power of cartoonists was explicitly recognised by the authorities who started to employ their talents for propaganda purposes almost immediately after the war began. David Langdon, one of the most prolific wartime cartoonists, created Billy Brown of London Town for the London Passenger Transport Board. Fougasse (Kenneth Bird), who had contributed his first cartoon to *Punch* in 1916 and who became the magazine's art editor in 1937, was employed by the Ministry of Information early in the war to produce a series of posters, 'Careless Talk Costs Lives'. They were designed to prevent wagging tongues from revealing military secrets to spies and fifth columnists who were then believed to exist in greater numbers in Britain than they actually did. Hitler, who presented an easy target for cartoonists with his trim moustache and slick of hair over the left eye, appeared in the posters in the most unlikely places: under an exclusive dining table, in the luggage rack of a train. But these sponsored efforts may well have had much less effect on a nation, which was already increasingly resentful of officialdom and bureaucracy, than the unfettered work of individual cartoonists who had chosen to preserve their precious choice of independence and freedom to work and to criticise in their own way.

There had never been so many cartoons published in any previous war. The domestic and international demand for cartoons was by then so great that one cartoonist, Kem, produced no less than 3,000 political cartoons for newspapers and magazines in many different countries, including Greece, Morocco, and China, between 1939 and 1943, in addition to his other wartime duties. This great output, which was paralleled by that of many other cartoonists, resulted inevitably in much insipid and impotent work, lacking in invention. During the evacuation from Dunkirk, for instance, the *Punch* cartoonist, Bernard Partridge, even hauled out the old British lion again, looking a little mangy after so much misuse. The veteran cartoonist, Strube, who had joined the *Daily Express* in 1912, relied on the same metonymical circus for some of his effects, showing the British lion improbably raiding the eagle's nest, carefully labelled 'the Ruhr' so that viewers would not miss the message. His Little Man, in his spotted tie, waistcoat, and bowler hat, had been one of the brilliant innovations of the interwar years, one of the first representations of Everyman; but, by 1940, he already seemed a little dated as he steps out in his air raid warden's helmet with a soldier, a factory worker, and Churchill, who had been made prime minister a few days before. But the work of the best wartime

Kenneth Bird (1887–1965) chose to work under the pseudonym of **Fougasse** –

an improvised land mine of the First World War – to avoid confusion with another *Punch* artist with the same name. He was educated at Cheltenham College. In 1916, he contributed his first cartoon to *Punch*, entitled *War's Brutalising Influence*, which showed how a fashionable young subaltern was soon transformed into a tough veteran of the trenches.

Fougasse was one of the new generation of postwar *Punch* cartoonists who rejected the old naturalistic

style of drawing with an explanatory caption, exemplified by the work of Partridge, in favour of a terser, simplified drawing which spoke for itself. He was the art editor of *Punch* from 1937 to 1949 and editor from 1949 to 1953. His series of drawings, *Careless Talk Costs Lives*, which was done for the Ministry of Information, introduced his work to a much wider public during the Second World War. He published many collections of his cartoons in book form.

Right: One of the famous Fougasse posters of the Second World War

cartoonists, like that of Low or of Zec in the *Daily Mirror* still have great strength; they were often bold, brash, uncompromising statements, more posters than cartoons, selling their ideas to a mass audience and arousing feelings, hopes, and expectations which people had never previously known they possessed.

The Second World War, like most others, did not go according to prediction, with London an instant mass of flames and thousands of civilian casualties from high explosives and gas. Instead, nothing, or almost nothing, happened, except at sea. The French remained secure, as they thought, in their Maginot Line facing the Germans in their West Wall (or, Siegfried Line as the Allies preferred to call it), ready to fight the last war all over again. As the weeks passed and turned into months, there was a widespread belief that the war would be over by Christmas and a cheerful mood of cheeky optimism was epitomised in the song *(We're gonna Hang out) The Washing on the Siegfried Line*, which became so very popular during the phoney war that it was sung everywhere from exclusive London club to NAAFI canteen. The cartoonists, however, as in previous wars, were not so easily deluded. During the phoney war, Pont (Graham Laidler) began contributing a series of cartoons to *Punch* called 'Popular Misconceptions', with such titles as 'Life in the BEF', which was published on 13 December

Three of the series of Pont cartoons published by *Punch*

POPULAR MISCONCEPTIONS—LIFE IN THE B.E.F.

POPULAR MISCONCEPTIONS (IN GERMANY)—THE GERMANS

POPULAR MISCONCEPTIONS (IN GERMANY)—THE ENGLISH

| Chamberlain | Greenwood | Halifax | | Sinclair | Duff Cooper | Alexander | Eden | K. Wood |
| Churchill | Attlee | | Bevin | | Morrison | | Amery | |

"ALL BEHIND YOU, WINSTON"

1939. Pont did not live long enough to fulfil his early promise as he died in the following year from poliomyelitis at the age of thirty-two, having already acquired a high reputation as a cartoonist which has gone on increasing since.

When the war on land and in the air started in earnest on 10 May 1940, with the German invasion of the Low Countries, it was even more devastating than had ever been anticipated. In the previous month the Germans had occupied Denmark, unopposed, and had invaded Norway. British attempts to aid the Norwegians turned into a fiasco, revealing how little Britain was prepared for war. Chamberlain was blamed and on 10 May Churchill became prime minister, promising the nation in his first speech nothing but 'blood, toil, tears and sweat'. After all the long months of indecisive waiting and false anticipations, Churchill's determined and dynamic leadership helped to create a new sense of purpose and of unity, depicted by Low in his cartoon, *All Behind You Winston*. The mood was sombre, like many of the cartoons of the era, but resolute.

One disaster followed another in quick succession. Holland, neutral as it had been in the First World War, but

Above: The David Low cartoon published after Churchill became prime minister

mobilised in readiness since September 1939, was invaded at 4 am on 10 May 1940 and capitulated within five days. Queen Wilhelmina and her government fled to England to continue the fight. Within less than a fortnight, Belgium had also gone. King Leopold, who chose to remain in his country, was disavowed by his government, who also came to England. As the German panzers and the German infantry moved into these countries, they were quickly followed by the 'angels of peace' led by the bespectacled Himmler, who descended black and forbidding on the occupied countries clutching their death list and their instruments of savagery and torture.

With the British Expeditionary Force cut off from the main French army, Calais already gone, and an overwhelming German superiority in men, tanks, and tactical aircraft, there was no alternative but to evacuate the British troops from the beaches of Dunkirk in Operation Dynamo. Between 27 May and 3 June over 200,000 British troops and nearly 140,00 French soldiers, were transported to England in 860 ships including paddle steamers, ferry boats, and fishing smacks. They had to leave virtually all their tanks and guns and other heavy equipment in France, but they had been saved to fight another day. What could have been the greatest military defeat in British history was turned into a victory by British ingenuity, pragmatism, and pluck,

Below: Low's view of the evacuation from Dunkirk

TO FIGHT ANOTHER DAY

Sidney Strube (1891–1956) created in his 'Little Man' one of the first cartoon representatives of Everyman in modern times – the highly-taxed, uncomplaining, lower-middle-class gent who was the constant victim of politicians' machinations. A true Cockney, born within the sound of Bow Bells, he started work as a junior draughtsman with a furniture firm, but he was determined to be an artist and studied at the John Hassall School of Art in Kensington.

He became a freelance cartoonist in 1910 and two years later became a staff member of the *Daily Express,* where he continued to work until 1948 when ill health forced him to resign. During the First World War he served with the Artists' Rifles on the western front, but continued to send back cartoons to his newspaper.

Hitler's irresolution, and Goering's false boasts that his *Luftwaffe* could eliminate the BEF while it waited on the beaches. The British, always at their best when they are staring real disaster firmly in the face, were united in their defiance as they had never been since the days of the Napoleonic invasion scares; no longer a nation of separate, recognisable individuals, but, as they were depicted in the cartoons, indistinguishable elements in a common task. The Germans entered Paris on 14 June and within a week the French had signed an armistice at Compiègne. Not for the first time in its history, Britain stood alone. Many of the political cartoonists made play with the same obvious theme of the steel-helmeted soldier standing guard on the white cliffs facing occupied France.

The Battle of Britain began on 10 July with German air attacks on Channel shipping and ports, which continued for a month, followed by another month of all-out attacks on airfields in south-east England. Hitler had assembled a huge fleet of invasion barges in the French ports as Napoleon had done 135 years before, but just as Britain had been saved by the Navy in the past, so it was saved then by Fighter Command which destroyed 1,733 German planes for a loss of 915 of its own. On 17 September Hitler postponed his planned invasion and on 12 October he cancelled it, haunted

Left: 'Britain stands alone' – the Strube cartoon published in the *Daily Express* on 29 May 1940

Below: A cartoon by Leslie Illingworth who had joined the *Daily Mail* as political cartoonist at the outbreak of the war

"THAT'S AS FAR AS I GOT, ADOLF"

REVIEW OF 1942

no doubt by the spectre of another dictator's failure just as the spirits of many Britons had been uplifted and sustained by the same memory.

The next two years were ones of hard, unremitting struggle for Britain, with the blitz on so many of its major cities, the relentless fight against the enemy U-boats in the long Battle of the Atlantic, military defeats in Greece, Crete, and North Africa, and the rapid loss of Malaya, Hong Kong, and Singapore after the Japanese had attacked Pearl Harbor on 7 December 1941. The turning point for Britain came with the decisive victory of Montgomery's Eighth Army over Rommel's *Afrika Korps* at El Alamein in October 1942. Meanwhile, Hitler, who had invaded Russia in the previous year had failed to take Moscow, and by the end of 1942 his Sixth Army had been cut off at Stalingrad and was on the verge of surrender. Although there were still many hard battles to be fought in the North African desert, in the mountains of Italy, on the Normandy beaches, on the north German plain, and in the Burmese jungles, there were the first hints of hope and of victory, so that for almost the first time political cartoonists, like Illingworth in his *Review of 1942*, could allow themselves to smile in some triumph again.

Above: The war against Hitler was going better for the Allies by the end of 1942, which prompted this celebratory cartoon by Illingworth

There was far less hatred of the Germans in the political cartoons than there had been in the First World War. Hitler had been diminished in stature by cartoons, propaganda, and his own tantrums to a dangerously low level of significance which helped to conceal the true nature of his inhuman malignancy. The goose-stepping German troops, the swollen vanity of Goering, the absurd ambition of Mussolini with his stubbly chin, the short, twisted frame of Goebbels were all too fatally easy to caricature with much the same result. Real hatred in the cartoons was reserved for the apparent evils of the Fascist regimes, the deportations, the forced labour, the execution of hostages, the mass extermination of Jews in concentration camps – and also for the Japanese, who were invariably portrayed as small simian creatures with large protruding teeth as in *Son of Heaven* by Vicky, a Hungarian Jew who had fled from Berlin before the war and who had been appointed the political cartoonist of the *News Chronicle* in 1941.

The government, conscious of the power of political cartoonists to influence public opinion, kept a wary, anxious eye on their work throughout the war, though they were granted considerable freedom to criticise. During the blitz, for instance, Low showed a group of homeless people shivering in the cold streets while the luxury flats, which

Victor Weisz, or **Vicky**, (1913–1966) was one of several foreign cartoonists who have been able to endear themselves to the British. Born of Hungarian parents in Berlin, he studied art there and then began contributing caricatures to Berlin newspapers. A lifelong Socialist, he published his first anti-Hitler cartoon in 1928, before he came to power.

In 1935, Vicky left Germany for England. After working as a freelance, he was appointed staff cartoonist on the *News Chronicle* in 1941. He resigned in 1955, when the editor refused to publish one of his cartoons on Kenya. After working for the *Daily Mirror,* he joined the *Evening Standard* in 1958. He also worked regularly for the *New Statesman*.

Although Vicky was not a great draughtsman, he was a great newspaperman, bubbling over with ideas, who could work with great speed and facility. He is best remembered for his caricature of Harold Macmillan as 'Supermac'.

SON OF HEAVEN

they could not afford to rent, remained empty and tenantless. (The criticism was not entirely justified as the Duke of Westminster had offered many of his empty flats in the West End to the London County Council to house the homeless from the East End of London, most of whom preferred to shelter in the Tube.) When two German battleships, the *Scharnhorst* and the *Gneisenau* sailed through the Channel in defiance of both the Royal Navy and the RAF on 12 February 1942, Illingworth reflected the public sense of outrage in a cartoon showing a cold wind blowing through the English Channel. There are hundreds of other examples of the continuing liberty to criticise. Of all the daily newspapers,

Above: A Vicky cartoon published in the *News Chronicle* in 1942. The caption read: 'A savage, running amok, secures advantage of surprise'

only the *Daily Worker* was banned from 21 January 1941 to 7 September 1942, not for its cartoons alone, though there were some powerful attacks by the resident cartoonist, Chen, on members of the government, including Churchill and the Home Secretary, Herbert Morrison, who was caricatured as a 'Labour misleader'.

The *Daily Mirror*, which became the best-selling daily newspaper during the war, was threatened with closure. In the early months of 1942, the paper and its powerful cartoonist, Philip Zec, had been conducting a vigorous campaign for the more energetic prosecution of the war, with attacks on 'nincompoop' aristocrats, lack of all-out effort, and the failure to control the black market. Matters came to a head when the *Mirror* published a Zec cartoon on 6 March, showing a shipwrecked sailor on a raft with a caption reading: 'The price of petrol has been increased by one penny – Official.' Churchill misconstrued this as an attempt to induce merchant seamen not to go to sea, though its real purpose was to attack selfish, pleasure motoring which was not ended, tardily, until the following July. The newspaper was let off with a severe warning.

Below: The Zec cartoon which nearly got the *Daily Mirror* banned in 1942

"Have you such a thing as a dart-board here, Vecchio Uomo?"

Left: Jon's Two Types
reach Italy

The authorities were far more tolerant of social cartoons
about Service life, which consistently mocked authority,
bureaucracy, and 'bull' in the rich comic tradition of the
English caricature extending back to Gillray's ridicule of the
supplementary militia during the Napoleonic wars. But
what had been external and transitory then, ceasing abruptly
when invasion seemed imminent, was now integral and
durable. The men and women, virtually all civilians in
uniform, went on laughing at Service life, their own plight,
and officers and NCOs for the duration. It was a war without
heroes or heroics, except when some fighting had to be done.

The average British army officer was no stiff-necked,
goose-stepping member of the *Wehrmact*, though his men
may sometimes have seen him in that light, but an ordinary,
decent sort of chap, with no great military pretentions and a
yearning to return to civilian life. He wore his uniform not
with inordinate pride as the Germans did, but as a
temporary, enforced expedient, adapting it, as many Eighth
Army officers did, to a civilian style. The Two Types,
created by Jon, were the archetypes who, as Field-Marshal
Earl Alexander of Tunis said in his foreword to a collection
of these cartoons, were true both to life and to their times. As
the Two Types fought their way back and forth across the
desert, they dreamed nostalgically of home, of pubs which
appeared as mirages in the desert, of real beer and cigarettes,
and of matches that were guaranteed to strike. When the
Eighth Army invaded Italy, they were delighted to sample
the wine which flowed in abundance at every street corner
and to drink *strega* by the mugful; but soon the old nostalgia
returned for a game of darts in the local, for a newsagent who
sold *Punch* and not some unfunny, foreign publication, and

162

PERCY PRUNE, Pilot-Officer (from the collection at Ineyne Manor, Prune Parva, Sussex)

Above: The favourite
cartoon character of the RAF

these yearnings were accompanied, to their surprise, by a new nostalgia for the desert, with its brewing up of tea in the hot sunshine instead of drinking local wine in the Italian rain. The Two Types appealed not only to the civilians in uniform but also to many professionals of all ranks, including generals, many of whom like Alexander and Slim had learnt to come closer to their junior officers and men than brass hats had ever done before. The British were brave, determined fighters, and masters of improvisation, but they remained more undisciplined and individual than the soldiers of many foreign armies. They were 'at heart, anti-militarist', as Alexander stated in his foreword to Jon's cartoons, and they had a natural repugnance to 'any form of regimentation'.

It was the same spirit which made fighter pilots wear scarves with their uniform and leave the top buttons of their jackets undone. The RAF also had its own favourite cartoon character, the ever-cheerful but incompetent Pilot-Officer Percy Prune, who always tried so hard but never quite succeeded in avoiding disaster. There was a deliberate playing down of heroism in the RAF, which created its own brand of nonchalant and euphemistic speech, in which aircrew never died but only 'went for a Burton', and never crashed, but only had a 'prang'. David Langdon, who went through the ranks of the RAF before he was commissioned, had one of the most observant eyes for all the incongruities and absurdities of Service life, the sick parade marching smartly at the bawled commands of the sergeant to the medical centre, and also a great compassion for the occasional oppressions caused by Service life which were

Right: 'Who, *me*?' The two
words which summarised
for many 'erks' the injustices
of Service life. A David
Langdon cartoon

David Langdon (b. 1914) a prolific cartoonist who first achieved fame during the Second World War when he created Billy Brown of London Town, a series of cautionary posters aimed at helping the traveller during the 'blitz' for the then London Passenger Transport Board. He worked in the Architects' Department of the LCC until the outbreak of war, when he was posted to the London Rescue & Demolition Service. In 1941 he joined the ranks of the RAF and left in 1945 as a Squadron Leader. He drew many cartoons about Service life, which were distinguished by their great compassion for the ordinary airman and soldier.

Langdon has been a regular contributor to *Punch* since 1937 and is a member of the *Punch* 'Table'. He is one of the few British artists to have appeared frequently in the *New Yorker,* and has contributed a weekly news-strip to the *Sunday Mirror* since 1948.

experienced by many 'erks'. The Navy, with its longer tradition of self-mockery, was well practised in seeing the funny side of Service life.

Women, as in the First World War, played a much bigger part in the war than ever before. Conscription had been introduced in December 1941, for single women and for childless widows between the age of twenty and thirty and was extended later to single women between eighteen and fifty-one years of age. The Services, which included nearly 400,000 women by the end of the war, usually had more volunteers than they needed, so that most of the conscripted women were directed into the munition factories. There

Below: The favourite pin-up cartoon character of the war, created by Norman Pett, whose exploits were featured in the *Daily Mirror*

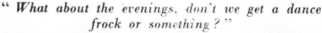

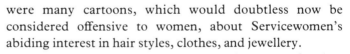

" What about the evenings, don't we get a dance frock or something ? "

Right: A Gilbert Wilkinson cartoon in the *Daily Herald* published before the days of Women's Liberation

were many cartoons, which would doubtless now be considered offensive to women, about Servicewomen's abiding interest in hair styles, clothes, and jewellery.

The woman who attracted most attention among Servicemen was Jane, the blonde cartoon character in the *Daily Mirror*, who was always getting into uniform as a Land Girl or as a canteen assistant, and by some mischance always getting out of it just as quickly again. Her adventures were followed with avidity by millions of Servicemen wherever the *Daily Mirror* could be obtained. Jane had her own special page in the *Daily Mirror*, but it also published daily a whole collection of strip cartoons featuring Buck Ryan, Beelzebub Jones, Belinda, Popeye, Ruggles, and Just Jake. Other daily newspapers had their own strip cartoons: Pop, who had first appeared in the *Daily Sketch* in 1921, Our Wilhelmina in the *Daily Express*, and the Arkubs in the *News Chronicle*.

There was an almost limitless demand for cartoon humour, which had already become such an integral part of everyday life that by the early thirties only four of the dozen or more daily and evening newspapers in London did not have its regular daily cartoon. They also featured prominently in the Services newspapers which became such a popular and characteristic feature of wartime life – *Parade*, the Middle East weekly first published in August 1940; the *Crusader*, published for the forces in the western desert in May 1942; the *Union Jack* which first appeared in September 1943; *Seac*, and the *Pacific Post*. All the commercial pocket-size magazines also had a great wealth of cartoons. Contributors to *Lilliput* included David Langdon, Osbert Lancaster, Bill Tait and 'haro', while *London Opinion* published both original work and reprinted cartoons from *Lilliput*, *Punch*, and other magazines. With the growth in the number of newspapers and magazines, and the new-found spirit of wartime unity, cartoons regained the universal appeal that they had not had since the Napoleonic wars. But their delights were no longer confined to a relatively small proportion of people living in cities. Modern technical means allowed them to be disseminated widely and quickly to all parts of the globe. Cartoons had never been studied more avidly by so many people as they were during the Second World War.

9

THE HOME FRONT

ven though some wealthy people sheltering in their 'funk holes' in the heart of the English countryside were able to evade the worst consequences of the war, most civilians were involved more deeply and suffered more severely than in any previous conflict. They were shouted at by officious air-raid wardens, rationed for food, regimented by identity cards, forced to save for post-war credits, conscripted into the mines and munition factories, bombed, 'doodle-bugged' and rocketed, and perpetually exhorted by the government and its agencies to do even more for the war effort. The war touched and altered so many different aspects of everyday life that it gave social cartoonists almost infinite scope in topic and invention. Like the trench-cartoonists of the First World War, they helped to sustain morale by translating the extraordinary into terms of normal life, reducing experience to assimilable proportions and giving hope of the return of more normal times. Lee, who had been doing a series of cartoons called 'London Laughs' for the *Evening News* changed the title to 'Smiling Through' when the war broke out, reflecting the change from instant amusement to patient fortitude, which was sorely needed by civilians during the war.

The blackout, which was universally loathed, produced the first great crop of wartime social cartoons. Two days before war was declared on 3 September 1939, the lights went out in city streets and country lanes and a total blackout was imposed in all private and public buildings and in most public vehicles. Motor cars were forbidden to use headlights and even their sidelights had to be heavily masked with the result that road deaths nearly doubled in the first months of war. The government was soon forced to introduce some minor relaxations. Glimmer or 'star' lighting cast down a single cone of light at main road intersections; drivers were allowed to use headlights with slitted, metal masks which gave narrow dipped rays of light; and pedestrians were permitted to use torches, masked with tissue paper, which produced the first of many great shortages of the war, as torch batteries, particularly the most popular No. 8 size, went under the counter. Cartoonists tried to introduce a little light into the nation's new tenebrous existence by making jokes about blackout encounters with irresistible objects, including members of the opposite sex, and about reserved English gentlemen in railway carriages who politely informed a fellow traveller that the platform was on the other side only after he had stepped out on to the rails.

As the rigours of the war increasingly disrupted normal life, almost everything started to go under the counter or on

Previous page:
Personalised gas-mask cases –
a *Punch* cartoon

168

Above: The aftermath
of the Liverpool blitz
of 5 May 1941

"*Ah, there's Mrs. Smith and her sister Mabel.*"

the ration – except for cartoon humour. Food rationing was introduced on 8 January 1940, initially of bacon (113 grams per person per week), butter (113 grams), and sugar (335 grams), though these amounts were later reduced and eventually many other foods including meat, tea, preserves, cheese, margarine and fats, tinned foods, and sweets were included. Other foods – fruit, fish, vegetables – also became scarce so that for a time even the humble onion virtually disappeared from the shops. The carrot became the great standby vegetable. Many untempting recipes were invented by the Ministry of Food for dishes such as carrot marmalade, carrot flan, and Woolton pie, named after the Minister of Food, which consisted of carrots, potatoes, and turnips baked with gravy and oatmeal under a pastry crust, if you had the fat to spare. There were long queues outside butcher's, fishmonger's, and greengrocer's shops, part-icularly if it was rumoured that some normally scarce food was temporarily available. Queueing became an accepted way of life especially for *Sociable Folk* who were just as interested in the gossip as the goods. Despite rationing, there

Left: *Punch* brings light – and laughter – to the blackout

Right: A Lee cartoon published in the *Evening News*

SOCIABLE FOLK.   " Oh, I don't want anything particular, but I think this is always such a nice CHATTY queue."

Left: A Gilbert Wilkinson cartoon satirising the 'Dig for Victory' campaign. The caption read: 'Maybe I am! But it's better than being a blinkin' pessimist!'

Below: Park railings had been removed to make armaments, but the conservative routine of life was still preserved. A *Punch* cartoon which had, and needed then, no caption

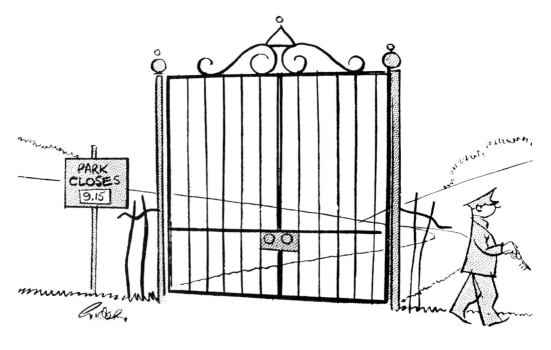

was a flourishing black market in food which produced another great crop of cartoons featuring fat, rich women in fur coats who outflanked the queue by entering the shop by the privileged back door and of hotel managers rebuking 'spivs' for bringing fresh salmon to the main door instead of the black market entrance at the rear. To supplement their meagre rations everyone started to dig for victory, as the government exhorted them to do, and to keep a few hens in their backyard to provide fresh eggs which had become an increasingly rare luxury.

Some of the shortages were deliberately self-imposed. After Lord Beaverbrook had been appointed Minister of Aircraft Production on 14 May 1940, he appealed to housewives to give up their aluminium pots and pans so that they could be used to make fighter aircraft. Many thousands of housewives emptied their kitchen shelves and cupboards in a patriotic gesture of sacrifice which they lived to regret later in the war when it became virtually impossible to replace them. Iron railings were removed from many parks and public buildings at the same time. As the war went on, more and more consumer goods started to disappear from the shops, provoking cartoons about shopkeepers who closed their premises for five minutes to do the annual stock-taking. Clothes rationing was introduced on 1 June 1941, with an initial allocation of sixty-six coupons, later reduced to forty, which was only sufficient to provide a woman with a mackintosh, a jacket, a skirt, a petticoat, and two pairs of stockings in a year. Women had to learn how to 'make do and mend' and to emulate or even to surpass the skills of the official propagandist 'Mrs Sew and Sew' by cutting pairs of Army surplus pants down to make warm winter knickers, by making petticoats from parachute silk, and by transforming dyed Army blankets into fashionable capes. By the beginning of 1942, the first Utility clothes, which were cheap and simple in style but well-cut, had appeared in the shops, and these were soon followed by Utility furniture which was also rationed. Household goods of all kinds became scarce as we can see in Sir Osbert Lancaster's pocket cartoon. These pocket cartoons were in themselves partly a product of another wartime scarcity – of newsprint, which reduced the size of papers to four broadsheet pages. Pocket cartoons, like Utility clothes and furniture, imposed new restraints and disciplines upon their creators with beneficial results in economy of style and caption.

There were hundreds of cartoons about the appalling difficulties of travel in wartime. Fearing that the railways would be unable to cope with their immense task of

A 'pocket' cartoon by Sir Osbert Lancaster

" Thaird floor ! No crockery, no hardware, no toys, and precious little baby linen ! "

Sir Osbert Lancaster
(b. 1908) is a man of many
parts who has made his mark
in many different fields as
well as cartoons. He was
educated at Charterhouse,
Lincoln College, Oxford, and
the Slade School of Art.
In 1938, he introduced the
pocket cartoon into the
William Hickey column of the
Daily Express and joined
the permanent staff and the
front page of the *Express* the
following year.

He is equally well-known
for his stage designs,
particularly for ballets, which
have been used in many
different countries. In
addition, he has designed
numerous operas for
Glyndebourne and the
London Opera Centre, and
has also worked for the
straight theatre. He is an
expert on Byzantine
architecture and is a prolific
writer not only of funny
books, but also of serious
works, and of send-ups of
architecture. Sir Osbert is
married to Anne Scott-
James, the writer and
journalist, and spends his
time between a flat in
London and a cottage in
Berkshire. He is a member of
several famous London
clubs.

When he was knighted in
1975, he became front-page
news in the *Daily Express*
with tributes from the staff
and a cartoon by Roy Ullyet.

Carl Ronald Giles
(b. 1916) is one of the most
popular and brilliant cartoonists of modern times,
whose squat figures are
invariably dominated by
their physical surround-
ings. He was trained
as an animated cartoonist
from 1930 to 1935 in various
London studios, before
he went to work as an
animator for Alexander
Korda in 1935. From 1937 to
1943, he worked as a
cartoonist on *Reynolds News,*
and then joined the *Sunday
Express* and the *Daily
Express,* where he has been
employed ever since. During
the Second World War he
was an official cartoonist
with the Second Army in
France, Belgium, Holland
and Germany. He was
awarded the OBE in 1959.

transporting troops, goods, and war materials, the government had seriously considered a plan to ration civilian rail
travel in the early months of the war, but fear of public
outrage persuaded them to abandon it. Official propagan-
dists then tried to make civilians feel guilty and unpatriotic
every time they stepped on to trains by displaying huge
posters, reading 'Is your journey really necessary?' at every
station. But these had little effect. There was always a dense
mass of civilians and Servicemen encumbered with rifles,
packs, and heavy kitbags waiting for the arrival of the train at
any main line station day and night. Travellers packed the
carriages and those who could not be accommodated were

forced to use the overhead luggage racks, the narrow corridors, the guard's van, even the lavatories. The trains were dirty, cold, uncomfortable, and slow, so that delays were occasionally measured not in hours but in days. There were hardly any restaurant cars and many station buffets were closed. The buses were also scarce, as many of them had to be taken off the road as there were neither spare parts to be had nor mechanics to repair them. Towards the end of 1942, buses stopped running at 9 pm in most provincial cities and very few ran on Sunday mornings. Petrol rationing for the private motorist had been introduced within three weeks of the outbreak of the war with a monthly allowance of four to ten gallons at 1s. 6d. a gallon, and pleasure motoring was abolished altogether in July 1942, when only essential users such as doctors and farmers were given a business allowance. In London, and in many big cities, taxis became increasingly scarce and they became even more difficult for the British to hire after the free-spending GIs had arrived.

From the beginning of 1942, when the first 3,000 American Servicemen arrived in Belfast, the free-spending GI (an acronym for Government Issue) increasingly made his presence felt both in ordinary life and in the cartoon world. The cartoon GI did not walk, but travelled by taxi which he alone could obtain; he did not march, but slouched

A *Sunday Express* cartoon by Giles

'I don't care if the war is nearly over—I'm not selling my cab for a fiver for a souvenir.'

or lounged; he did not salute, but gave a friendly wave. His image was scarcely any different from reality as British cartoons have always been based just as much on observation as imagination.

But the most prolific source of cartoon humour on the home front was the blitz which, contrary to all military expectations, increased the morale of the British people and gave them a spirit of defiant unity which they had never had before and which they have never yet recaptured since. London had been bombed by Zeppelins and aircraft during the First World War, but they were small hit-and-run affairs which did relatively little damage and caused few civilian deaths, only a thousand or so in all. The blitz on London and other major cities, deliberately designed to cause the greatest terror and number of deaths among civilians, was completely new in military history and different in kind from the artillery bombardments of besieged garrison towns in previous wars. The Germans had first tried out their murderous policy of the indiscriminate bombing of civilians when their Condor Legion bombed the small town of Guernica on 27 April 1937, a market day, during the Spanish Civil War. In the first month of the Second World War, the *Luftwaffe* had killed thousands of civilians and destroyed much of the city in their raids on Warsaw. On 14 May 1940, the Germans had bombed Rotterdam and destroyed an eighth of the city, even though surrender negotiations were in progress. But the blitz on Britain was the first time that an uninvaded country had been subjected to such a sustained and ferocious bombardment from the air.

Cartoonists played a major part in helping the British people to keep smiling through the blitz. Much of their work was defensively humorous, a shield against fate, a quizzical look at the tendency of human character and social convention to reassert itself even in the most adverse circumstances, so that the little old lady asks through the bomb-blasted window if the shop is still open and the auxiliary fireman politely knocks at the front door of the ruined home before entering. Cartoonists made fun of the gas masks which had been issued to 38,000,000 civilians after Munich, with special, gaily-painted 'Mickey Mouse' masks for children under five, and gas helmets for babies with a concertina-type pump for their mothers to operate. There were many jokes about the Anderson shelters which swelled up monstrously in backyards and about the Morrison shelters, consisting of a steel-topped table with wire mesh sides, which were introduced in March 1941.

A few days after the blitz had started on 7 September 1940,

Right: A cartoon by Hewitt published in *Punch*

"Don't stand there knocking, Roberts, GO STRAIGHT IN."

"By the way, did you remember to feed the canary?"

"What did I tell you? Give them an inch and they take a mile."

"Congratulations, Herr Professor! Our Fuehrer will now think up something for it to do."

Above left: A Sillince
cartoon satirising
the introduction of the
Morrison indoor shelters

Above: The invention of
the V1 flying bomb provoked
this Emett cartoon in *Punch*

Left: A blitz cartoon
by Brockbank

there was an underground migration from the East End to the West End of London as thousands of people from the blitzed dock area sought safety in the shelter of the Tube. Initially, the authorities tried to stop people sleeping in the Underground at night, but people evaded the ban by buying a ticket and refusing to come out after the last train had left. Within days, many Tube stations were packed with shelterers every night and the authorities soon accepted the inevitable and provided bunk beds, canteens, and concerts. Morale remained so high during the blitz, which lasted until the middle of May 1941, that the majority of Londoners, some sixty per cent, did not even bother to go to a shelter of any kind, but went to bed in the normal way or spent the night downstairs sleeping on the settee or squatting beneath the stairs.

They displayed an equal nonchalance later in the war, when Hitler launched his secret weapons in a desperate attempt to restore his shattered prestige and his failing fortunes. The first V1, a pilotless, jet-propelled plane carrying about a ton of high explosive, was launched on 13

June 1944, and about another 10,000 followed. There were many cartoons about V1s, which failed to cause the fear and panic among Londoners which Hitler had anticipated. Londoners soon got so used to the cutting-out of the engine and the eerie silence before the plane crashed, that many people didn't even bother to look up at them any more. By the time the V1 attacks ended in August, about seventy per cent were being destroyed in the air by fighter planes or anti-aircraft fire. On 8 September the Germans introduced an even more powerful weapon, the V2 rocket, which could only be countered by bombing the launching sites. About 1,000 rockets were launched, but Londoners soon learnt to live with them too, believing fatalistically that death would have come before you heard the fatal explosion. These final, desperate attacks on the civilian population were shrugged off by the people and the cartoonists, for the end of the war in Europe was obviously in sight.

Meanwhile, on the other side of the world, the 'forgotten' Fourteenth Army had been fighting its way back into Burma, capturing Rangoon from the Japanese on 2 May 1945, and the Americans had been fighting one bloody battle after another to regain control of islands in the Pacific as they advanced towards the Japanese mainland, which was already being heavily attacked from the air. The Japanese surrendered on 14 August 1945, after an atomic bomb had been dropped on Hiroshima and another on Nagasaki. Relief at the ending of the most devastating war in history overshadowed concern over the means which had been employed. In the *Sunday Express*, Giles showed two Japanese sitting in the bomb-blasted rubble and questioning whether their emperor was really the Son of Heaven. In *Punch*, E. H. Shepherd depicted an angel and the devil poised about a fiery ball of atomic energy while Low employed a similar theme, showing a mad-looking scientist holding out a ball, marked life or death, to a child, labelled humanity, who is crawling towards him over the surface of the globe. But the possible consequences of these fatal acts of war remained too momentous for easy or quick assimilation – or, for that matter much humour.

EPILOGUE

"Feelthy Conference . . ."

Britain emerged from the Second World War, triumphant, forward-looking, determined to create a fairer society, a better world, but so gravely weakened and exhausted by its participation in the war, which was longer and more total than that of any other nation, that it was unable to sustain these noble ambitions. The human cost of the war had been less than the First World War, although still severe, with 300,000 members of the armed forces, 60,000 civilians, and 30,000 merchant seamen killed. The financial cost, however, was much greater. In its worldwide struggle to preserve freedom, Britain had been reduced to beggary with a massive increase of £3,000 million in its overseas debts much of it owed to nations which had been initially reluctant to enter the fight; its exports and its invisible earnings more than halved; its merchant fleet reduced to two-thirds of its pre-war size; its industries run down; its cities destroyed; and many of its surviving homes bare and shabby. No other country had made so many sacrifices, not only in its own interests, but also for other nations, or had received so much gratitude in words, but so little tangible reward or recompense, apart from Marshall Aid, which, however, was also provided for the former enemy countries of Germany and Italy.

After the war, for the first time in its history, Britain did not immediately allow its armed forces to wither away. To cope with the country's continuing global military commitments and the growing threat from Russia as international relations froze icily into a cold war, Britain made a radical break with tradition in 1947 when it decided to retain conscription in peacetime. National Servicemen were called up at the age of eighteen to serve for an eighteen-month period which was later extended to two years.

In the post-war period, British armed forces have been more actively engaged in world-wide duties than in any previous period of peace. In the long retreat from empire, the Forces have been involved in a large number of peacekeeping operations in many different parts of the world, including Cyprus, Hong Kong, Kenya, Aden, and Sarawak. British Servicemen have been stationed in West Germany ever since the end of the war, initially as forces of occupation and later as allies of the former enemy. The nuclear deterrent has helped to prevent the outbreak of global war, though there have been many insurrections, guerrilla, and conventional wars in some of which Britain has been involved: the fight against Communist guerrillas in Malaya from 1948 to 1960, the Korean war from 1950 to 1953, and the war between Israel and Egypt in 1956.

Previous page: The Suez crisis provoked this Ronald Searle cartoon in *Punch*, with Nasser offering his own terms to delegates to the international conference

Right: 'Kiss me goodnight, sergeant-major', National Servicemen try their hand at arms drill somewhere in England in 1954

182

Apart from some mandatory gestures, cartoonists have tended to ignore most of these conflicts, being more preoccupied with political affairs and social changes at home. The only conflict which aroused any of the old passion and fervour was the Anglo-French intervention in the Israel-Egypt war. Relations between Egypt and the West started to deteriorate after Colonel Nasser decided to buy arms from Czechoslovakia in 1955. When Britain and the United States withdrew their offer of aid for the building of the High Dam on the Nile, Nasser, in retaliation, nationalised the Suez Canal so that he could use the profits to pay for the project. Anthony Eden who had become prime minister after waiting in the wings for so many years, completely misjudged the situation, believing that the Egyptians would be unable to run the canal, that Nasser was another Hitler, and that the Americans, the senior partner in the western alliance, would tolerate the use of force to seize the canal.

When diplomatic negotiations foundered, the British government called up 30,000 reservists and requisitioned merchant ships. On 29 October 1956, Israel attacked Egypt and quickly seized the Sinai peninsula and the Gaza strip. The following day, Britain and France warned both Israel and Egypt to withdraw their forces 16 kilometres from the canal. Egypt rejected the ultimatum. On 31 October in the guise of peace-makers but almost certainly in collusion with the Israelis, Britain and France attacked Egypt, seizing Port Said, and advancing almost halfway up the canal before they were halted on 6 November by the threat of economic sanctions by the United States, the opposition of other allies, and a resolution of the General Assembly of the United Nations condemning their action.

Britain was more deeply divided by the Suez affair than by any other foreign crisis in its post-war history. Many sections of the press were critical. *Punch* published a cartoon by Illingworth showing Eden leading a body of troops over the brow of a hill, with a caption based on the nursery rhyme about the Duke of York:

> *The grand old Anthony Eden*
> *Recalled thirty thousand men;*
> *He marched them up to the top of a hill*
> *And he'll march them down again.*

This, with a significant change of emphasis, brings us back to where we started in the French revolutionary wars. It is, however, no longer the unfortunate military commander, the Duke of York, who is lampooned, but the incompetent and ineffectual Prime Minister who, weakened by illness,

Left: The Illingworth cartoon about the Suez crisis published in *Punch*

criticism, and the strains of office, resigned within a couple of
months of the Suez fiasco of his own creation. The finger had
turned to point at politicians, not generals. More than
twenty years of continuous civilian involvement in the
armed forces in both war and peace had helped to create a
climate for much better understanding between civilians and
the Services and to bridge the gap which had existed for so
many centuries.

There has been some slight widening of the gulf since.
Conscription was abolished in 1960 so that Britain once
again became the only European power without conscripts,
except for Luxembourg whose total forces are so minimal
that their absence has been scarcely noticed. Britain's armed
forces, slimmed down in size, have been banished to the
wings, unless they are given some thankless task by
politicians in Northern Ireland, but they are accepted as
essential members of the cast to a much greater extent than
they have ever been. They no longer feature much in the
cartoons; there are no more drawing room captains, toy
soldiers, or Colonel Blimps, since cartoonists have found
other, more profitable figures of fun.

During the last two centuries, cartoonists have provided a
unique picture of the nation's involvement in wars both
great and small, from the great global conflict with France
which opened the period to the two devastating wars with
Germany which brought it to an end, and all the minor
expeditions and engagements in between. It is a record of
which Britain can be proud for no other foreign government
has allowed its pictorial critics to mock and deride the most
sensitive aspects of its authority – the armed forces and
national defence – with such uninhibited and unrestricted
licence for such a long, uninterrupted period of time. There
have been remarkably few prohibitions or punishments – the
fining of the *Bystander* for publishing a cartoon of an
intoxicated soldier during the First World War and the
banning of the *Daily Worker* for a time during the Second
World War, though that was occasioned far more by the
paper's support of a People's Convention for a People's
Peace than its anti-government cartoons.

No other nation has possessed such a great gift of laughing
at itself so uproariously and consistently over such a long
period of time, which may have robbed it of some
competitiveness, but has also been a great source of inner
strength, particularly in times of war, when the British sense
of humour has always been its most effective secret weapon.
During the First World War, for instance, the German
cartoons were much more stiff and scornful and the French

were far more exalted and heroic, which was why they wanted to borrow Bruce Bairnsfather to create a down-to-earth Old Bill for them. Such a loan would have been less than revolutionary in Britain, where so many of the greatest cartoonists have been foreign, from the *Vanity Fair* caricaturist Carlo Pellegrini, to the Australian Will Dyson, the New Zealander David Low, and the Hungarian Jew Vicky. The British have laughed with them just as much, or even more, than they have with their own native cartoonists in a tolerant contemplation of their own shortcomings and defects which no other nation has yet learnt to match.

SELECT BIBLIOGRAPHY

Adam, H.Pearl, *International Cartoons of the War*, Chatto and Windus, 1916

Armstrong, Anthony, *Prune's Progress*, pictured by RAFF, Herbert Jenkins n.d.

Ashbee, C.R., *Caricature*, Chapman and Hall, 1928

Ashton, John, *English Caricature and Satire on Napoleon I*, Chatto and Windus, 1884

Bairnsfather, Bruce, *Wide Canvas*, John Long, 1939

Bradshaw, Percy V., *They Make us Smile*, Chapman and Hall, 1942

Broadley, A.M. and Rose, J.Holland, *Napoleon in Caricature*, John Lane, 1911, 2 vols

Daily Mirror Newspapers, *Jane at War*, Wolfe Publishing, 1976

Fougasse, *. . . And the Gatepost*, Chatto and Windus, 1940

Fuchs, Eduard, *Der Weltkrieg in der Karikatur*, Albert Langen, Munich, 1916

Geipel, John, *The Cartoon*, David and Charles, Newton Abbot, Devon, 1972

George, M.Dorothy, *English Political Caricature*, 1793–1832, Oxford University Press, Oxford, 1959

George, M.Dorothy, *Hogarth to Cruikshank, Social Change in Graphic Satire*, Allen Lane, Penguin Press, 1967

Gifford, Denis, *Victorian Comics*, Allen and Unwin, 1976

Grego, Joseph, *Rowlandson, The Caricaturist*, Chatto and Windus, 1880, 2 vols

Grego, Joseph, *The Works of James Gillray*, Chatto and Windus n.d.

Hill, Draper, *The Satirical Etchings of James Gillray*, Dover Publications, New York, 1976

Hillier, Bevis, *Cartoons and Caricatures*, Studio Vista, 1970

Hollowood, Bernard, *Pont*, Collins, 1969

Jon, *The Two Types*, Benn 1960, foreword by Field-Marshal Earl Alexander of Tunis

Kem, *Lines of Attack*, Alliance Press n.d.

Lancaster, Osbert, *Assorted Sizes*, John Murray, 1944

Langdon, David, *All Buttoned Up!*, Collins, 1940

Langdon, David (ed) *Punch with Wings*, Arthur Barker n.d.

Low, David, *Political Parade*, Cresset Press n.d.

Low, David, *Years of Wrath*, Gollancz, 1949

National Portrait Gallery, *Drawn and Quartered*, Times Newspapers, 1970

Pont, *The British Carry On*, Collins, 1940

RAFF and Armstrong, Anthony, *Nice Types*, Methuen, 1943

Robb, Brian, *My Middle East Campaigns*, Collins, 1944

Searle, Ronald, *Forty Drawings*, Cambridge University Press, Cambridge, 1946

Sullivan, Edmund J., *The Kaiser's Garland*, Heinemann, 1915

Tait, *Tait Smiles*, Scoop Books, Glasgow n.d.

Vicky, *Cartoons*, Walding Press, 1944

Westwood, H.R., *Modern Caricaturists*, Lovat Dickson, 1932

Wheeler, H.F.B., and Broadley, A.M., *Napoleon and the Invasion of England*, John Lane, 1908, 2 vols

Wilkinson, Gilbert, *What a Life*, Odhams Press n.d.

ACKNOWLEDGMENTS

The publishers wish to thank the following for their kind permission to use their illustrations:

BBC Hulton Picture Library: pp. 29, 33, 46 (both), 47 (top), 76–7, 87, 106, 115, 121, 147, 148 (bottom), 159 (bottom), 164 (top), 174 (both), 183. British Library: pp. 32, 49, 78, 80, 81, 83, 84, 88, 91, 93, 96, 98, 101, 104, 107, 112, 113, 117, 119, 132, 135, 137, 139, 140, 143 (bottom), 156 (bottom), 157, 158, 160, 162, 163 (both), 165 (top), 171, 172 (top), 173, 175. British Museum: pp. 12 (bottom), 13, 14–15, 18, 20, 25, 28, 33, 35, 41, 51, 53. Mary Evans Picture Library: p. 21. Imperial War Museum: pp. 125, 127, 129, 151 (bottom). London Express News Service: pp. 156 (top). Sir David Low, by kind permission of the London Evening Standard and the Low Trustees: pp. 145, 148 (top), 154, 155. Mansell Collection: pp. 6, 9, 47 (bottom), 56, 126–7, 131, 168–9. E. J. Martin: pp. 38–9. Mirror Group Newspapers: pp. 161, 164 (bottom). From the copy in the Mitchell Library, Sydney: p. 143 (top). National Army Museum: pp. 12 (top), 95, 110, 123. National Maritime Museum: pp. 26–7, 40, 43, 52. *Punch*: Frontispiece, pp. 37, 48, 55, 60, 62, 64, 65, 66, 67 (both), 69, 70, 72, 73, 75, 94, 109, 114–15, 120, 128, 142, 151 (top), 152, 153 (both), 167, 170, 171 (bottom), 177, 178 (both), 179, 181, 184. Oliver Heath Robinson: p. 138. Roger Viollet: pp. 10–11.

Front jacket: British Museum (centre), *Punch* (all others).
Back jacket: British Museum.

INDEX

A Wallis Mills. 1914.

Tommy (to his pal in middle of charge). "Lo